RETHINKING CHURCH MUSIC

(Revised and Enlarged)

Paul W. Wohlgemuth

Foreword by Don G. Fontana

HOPE PUBLISHING COMPANY

Carol Stream, Illinois 60187

Dedicated with love and appreciation
to my wife
BARBARA

Acknowledgment
Appreciation is expressed to publishers who have granted
the privilege of using their copyrighted materials, to students and colleagues who have shared insights, to Douglass
C. Percy who helped prepare the original publication, and
to Lynn M. Nichols who so competently proofread the new
manuscript.

Contents

Foreword

One of the most important needs of the Christian today is to know more about church music—the music used by God in the revelation of His truths and wisdom. The Christian church is besieged with numerous styles of music that intend to communicate the gospel message to multi-levels of intellectual, musical and social strata. One quickly discovers that there is no one "all-encompassing" musical style, rather, there are many musical idioms and styles used to reach the broadest possible segment of the churched and non-churched society. Though labels change from decade to decade, century to century, still one is quickly made aware that God constantly and consistently inspires authors and composers to write new and meaningful spiritual expressions for the nurturing, edifying and admonishing of His children.

To have a knowledge of the beginnings of church music, as recorded throughout scripture, and to trace the development of the numerous forms of textual and musical expression, particularly since the reformation, places in perspective and expands levels of tolerance, understanding and personal appreciation for the contemporary efforts of today.

The Christian lay person and church musician alike can learn and appreciate church music at a new level through this outstanding literary contribution—"Rethinking Church Music".

This book, written by Dr. Paul W. Wohlgemuth, one of the nation's foremost leaders in the area of church music, is designed to bring into focus the broad concept of church music, tracing it from the beginnings, considering it as a vehicle in the act of Christian worship and finally examining it in the light of current use in today's Christian experience.

Dr. Wohlgemuth has an impressive background of training, teaching, performing and music ministry leadership. He is eminently qualified to properly and sensitively deal with the pertinent and timely topic "Rethinking Church Music".

I am most pleased to commend this important volume to you and I know the succeeding pages will bring instruction, insight, enlightenment, inspiration and a strong foundation for future contemplation, thought and action.

Don G. Fontana
Crystal Cathedral
January—1981

Preface

Every person carries a musical posture with him when he walks, plays, studies, or worships. Music, or lack of it, affects every aspect of life. As you read these chapters, keep your mind and heart open, since the Lord may want you to experience something new. My words may not stimulate or enlighten, but God may!

These are not chapters on music theory and appreciation, discussions of classical sacred music, or stories about how different hymns were written. Instead, this book deals with current issues in church music, the relationship of music to our worship, and the urgency of relating a timeless gospel to a contemporary society. Since the initial discussion on church music has to do with broad Christian precepts, many of the suggestions and principles given in this book are equally applicable to Christian education, missions, and the ministry.

I would feel more comfortable directing a choir than writing about music, but I feel a need exists for more discourse on church music. It is possible to be well informed in many facets of education and Christian truth and at the same time to be abysmally ignorant in another area—and I believe that *one* is often church music! I once heard of a highly-degreed history professor who knew two songs: one was "Dixie" and the other wasn't!

Since I draw much of my material from personal experience, a brief personal glimpse into my background and my testimony will help the reader to understand the context of my concerns.

I was born into a Christian family in the small rural town of Fairview, Oklahoma. My commitment to Jesus Christ was made during a week of revival meetings conducted by the Reverend Theodore Epp, pastor of the "Back to the Bible" radio program. As a member of the Mennonite Brethren Church, I have enjoyed a rich and fruitful life of Christian service.

The relationship of my work in church music to my personal life was brought into sharp focus several years ago when my brother Wesley died at 42, leaving a beautiful testimony of Christian faith. During the months that followed, my wife and I found ourselves awake many nights, thinking, praying, and asking ourselves, "What really counts in our lives? Wesley's earthly life is over. What part of his life was straw and what was gold?" After a thorough reassessment of my own primary goals and ambitions, my life began to change.

The searching questions I asked then still influence me today. As a result, I have kept that keen realization that none of us can afford to say that life is boring or that there is nothing to do. I have reached a new awareness of the meaning of "redeeming the time," especially for those who work in the ministry of church music.

I

Music in the Church: Bane or Blessing?

We need to recognize that we are not the first to face changing days. Tensions of all types have always existed in the church. During its history, the church has sought to express its faith in language, art, music, architecture, and sculpture. Christians through the centuries have been reassessing the role of music in the life of the church. They have sought to determine whether their music was a source of harm or help, bane or blessing.

The sound of music is prominent in our land today. The mass media provide the means to disseminate music on such an extensive scale that nearly everyone is influenced by it, even though the musical diet it provides is almost entirely popular music. This one-sided exposure has created a nation of listeners who base their appreciation of music on feeling rather than on intellect. The result is a type of existential listening that has contributed to a superficial understanding of the function of church music.

A person's past distasteful experience with music, lack of exposure to a variety of music, and simple prejudice and ignorance about music present formidable barriers to a meaningful musical experience in his personal life. On the other hand, moderate familiarity with the language of music, an inquisitive mind, a learning spirit, and a search for meaning make our spiritual quest more thrilling and our Christian life more abundant.

As a backdrop for considering the role of music, an evaluation of church music practices from the historical, psychological, and biblical points of view will be helpful.

Historical

The Christian church community was born in the setting of its ancestral Jewish faith. It carried on the tradition of using music in its religious services as had its forefathers in Old Testament days. Now that the Messiah, Jesus of Nazareth, had come, songs of joy were shared in their worship services. The New Testament speaks of the use of music in worship and in daily experience.

We read that Jesus ate with His disciples in the upper room and "when they had sung an hymn, they went out into the mount of Olives" (Matt. 26:30). Paul and Silas also sang praises to God as they sat in their dark dungeon (Acts 16:25). The apostle Paul exhorted the Colossian church to teach and admonish one another in psalms and hymns and spiritual songs (Col. 3:16).

As the Christian church grew and dispersed, its music went with it. Often the worship service developed into an elaborate form that used the music of the day. But because communication among the churches was limited, a uniform program of the use of music in worship did not develop. Church music became confusing and, in the opinion of many church leaders, a hindrance to public worship. As a result, the Council of Laodicea, A.D.343–381, outlawed congregational singing. The Council decreed that only specially appointed singers could present music in the church services. The church in its early history had found some music to be a bane and some a blessing.

By the time the Reformation swept Europe during the sixteenth century, polyphonic music, musical notation, and the printing press had developed. As people found a new life in Jesus Christ, they felt the urge to express their praise and thanksgiving in song. Fortunately, Martin Luther understood the possibilities of the use of music and gave singing back to the congregation in its own language. Out of this developed one of the great hymn forms for congregational singing, the chorale.

But music by itself was not enough. It needed the human instrument: men and women of vision with a willingness and desire to work and a reasonable understanding of the procedure and materials they were using. Reformation music became a blessing to the people because of Martin Luther's positive attitude toward music as an effective tool to nurture his congregation. He also found it useful in teaching doctrine and religious principles. This attitude reflected itself as he exalted the role of congregational singing without diminishing the function of the organ. His outspoken view on the excellence of church music included both the simple chorale and the more elaborate musical settings for choir and organ. The following quotations from Luther's writings reveal the importance he placed on church music in his ministry.

I have always loved music. Those who have mastered this art are made of good stuff, and are fit for any task. It is necessary indeed that music be taught in the schools. A teacher must be able to sing; otherwise I will not so much as look at him.[1]

Following the example of the prophets and fathers of the Church, we intend to collect German psalms for the people so that through the medium of song the Word of God may remain among the people.[2]

I am not ashamed to confess publicly that next to theology there is no art which is the equal of music, for she alone, after theology, can do what otherwise only theology can accomplish, namely, quiet and cheer up the soul of man.[3]

Not all significant music of the Reformation centered on Luther. John Calvin in France and Ulrich Zwingli in Switzerland also gave leadership to the Reformed church. After observing the singing of Lutheran congregations in Strasbourg, Calvin became convinced that spiritual vitality could be nurtured in singing and that songs should be incorporated into the worship service. In contrast to Luther, Calvin sanctioned the Psalms as the only text suitable for congregational singing; additionally, he had a distaste for hymns and denied the power of the Holy Spirit to inspire men afresh in the praise of God. Calvin also opposed part

[1]Robert M. Stevenson, *Patterns of Protestant Church Music* (Durham, N.C.: Duke U., 1953), pp. 6–7.

[2]Karl Anton, *Luther and die Musik* (Zwickau: 1928), p. 25, cited by Walter E. Buszin, "Luther on Music," *Musical Quarterly* 32 (January 1946):87.

[3]Anton, cited by Buszin, pp. 83–84.

singing and the use of musical instruments. Nevertheless, his views on the use of music encompassed a positive persuasion. He states in his famous *Institutio* of 1536:

> If the singing come not from the heart it is worth nothing, and can only awaken God's wrath. Singing in itself is good and useful; our tongues must praise God, and as we honour Him by a common faith, we must also unite in glorifying Him before men that they may hear our confession of His name and be inspired with the desire of following our example. Singing in the church has been practised from the earliest times; the Apostle Paul recommended the use of spiritual songs. But neither the ear nor the spirit must be distracted. . . . With proper moderation, therefore, the use of singing is holy and useful. Those melodies which are introduced merely to give pleasure are not agreeable to the majesty of the Church and must be infinitely displeasing to God.[4]

As a result of John Calvin's inspiration, many metrical settings were given to the Psalms. The psalter now gave worshiping Christians the opportunity to sing their joys, praises and petitions to God. The influence of the psalter became a part of the Reformation as it swept across continental Europe and into England. Various psalters were published, including Sternhold-Hopkins (Old Version), Tate and Brady (New Version), Ravenscroft and Este.

Yet by the middle of the seventeenth century, Christians in England became indifferent to Psalm singing. In his *Musick's Monument,* published in 1676, Thomas Mace stated: "Tis sad to hear what whining, toting, yelling or screeching there is in many country congregations."[5] In the minds of some church leaders Psalm singing had become a bane, and many like Bishop Cranmer removed congregational singing from the liturgy. Hoping to improve this situation, men like Thomas Ken, George Herbert, and

[4]Thomas Young, *The Metrical Psalms and Paraphrases* (London: A. & Black, 1909), pp. 16–17.

[5]Albert Edward Bailey, *The Gospel in Hymns* (New York: Scribner's, (1950), p. 88.

Joseph Addison began to write hymns for congregational singing. Their work, however, was not generally accepted. Many persons still felt that hymns were unscriptural and inappropriate.

At the beginning of the eighteenth century Isaac Watts gave to England the hymns that recharged congregational singing with new fervor and interest. Through his writing of *Psalms Imitated* and *Hymns of Human Composure,* he bridged the gap between the singing of psalms to the singing of hymns. Because of this, Watts has become known as the father of English hymnody. His hymns have blessed the English-speaking world and are still sung today. Perhaps his best-loved hymn is the reverent and worshipful "When I Survey the Wondrous Cross." Hymns like this gave hymnology its rightful place in worship.

With this breakthrough in the development of English hymnody, the way was prepared for the two brothers, John and Charles Wesley, to give the English hymn the impetus that lifted congregational singing to new heights of enthusiasm, joy, and meaning. The significance of their contributions to church music is the hymn compilations and hymn translations of John Wesley and more than 6,500 original hymns credited to Charles Wesley.

During the nineteenth century a great number of English hymns were written among all Christian groups. Of interest were the emerging movements of the Young Men's Christian Association, Salvation Army, Sunday schools, and mass evangelism that created a need for a new song that would be different from the Victorian hymns and those of Watts and the Wesleys, and that could easily be sung by the masses. Out of this need arose the gospel song. The Moody-Sankey revivals gave the gospel songs the impetus they needed to become an effective tool for evangelism, missions, testimony, and Christian development. Out of this movement also came the gospel chorus, used especially by children and young people.

By mid-twentieth century the folk hymn gained immense popularity even though it had been around for many years. During the 1960's and 1970's, there emerged new types of scripture songs and renewal songs set to a conflicting mixture of moderately contemporary as well as jazz and rock styles. Time will tell which styles will be a bane or a blessing.

Psychological

The power of music has more influence than is usually understood. It can amuse, control moods, arouse tears, and incite action. It can debauch or delight, kill or cure, bring darkness or light. Plato and Aristotle even legislated against the promiscuous use of music.

The experience of Saul and David points up the power of music:

> And Saul's servants said unto him, Behold now, an evil spirit from God troubleth thee. Let our lord now command thy servants, which are before thee, to seek out a man, who is a cunning player on an harp: and it shall come to pass, when the evil spirit from God is upon thee, that he shall play with his hand, and thou shalt be well. And it came to pass, when the evil spirit from God was upon Saul, that David took an harp, and played with his hand: so Saul was refreshed, and was well, and the evil spirit departed from him (I Sam. 16:15–16, 23).

The world also has discovered its power. Today, youth's permissive lifestyle and the extensive use of drugs are closely allied to music. Note the programming of rock festivals and their attendant evils.

The mass media use music extensively in various forms. Much care is given to the preparation of effective background music for television advertisements, programs, and cartoons.

Television music often is cataloged under descriptive terms such as chase music, comical music, running music, and walking music. Background music for motion pictures is also given critical evaluation. The multimillion-dollar recording industry makes powerful and persuasive tools of the juke box, cassette, and stereo phonograph.

Music in society has not been confined strictly to channels of entertainment. Medicine has made great progress in harnessing the power of music for therapeutic uses. Research has shown that musical stimuli produce direct physical reactions such as dilation of the eyes, changes in blood pressure, pulse, and glandular secretions. Music therapy is an accepted procedure used by the healing arts in mental hospitals.

Some years ago, Dr. E. Thayer Gaston of the University of Kansas demonstrated the effect of music upon human expression. In an experiment, graduate art students were asked to paint anything that came to mind for a period of time as music was played. After the first period was concluded and a rest break taken, they came back for another session and followed precisely the same procedure. The only variable was that the music played was vastly different for the two sessions. During one session a contemporary composition was played using harsh dissonances, contemporary chords, heavy rhythms, and a great variation of dynamic levels. In the other session the music was taken from the impressionistic period, with its smooth, flowing harmonic and melodic style. During the session when contemporary music was played, most students painted with sharp, angular lines. Their colors were contrasts of blacks and reds, and the forms were distorted, unbalanced, asymmetrical, and often confusing. By contrast, the pictures painted during the impressionistic music session showed the use of pastels, pastoral and water scenes, smooth lines, and blending textures. This experiment indicates that music does affect our actions and thought patterns.

Music is often the catalyst for intense situations. Such an incident was experienced by the concert choir of the University of Southern California. The singers were just finishing a long dress rehearsal for a spring concert when the director realized that they had forgotten to rehearse one number. Reassembling the weary singers, he directed them through the remaining piece, Tschesnikoff's "Let Thy Holy Presence." Something of the magic of the anthem touched the chorale, and they all left the auditorium in a quiet, reverent spirit. A single anthem was able to stir deep changes in the tired minds and bodies of the choir members.

On another occasion, as the cathedral choir of the Hollywood Presbyterian Church sang the morning anthem, the Spirit of God moved among the people, making it apparent that something unusual was happening. After the choir had finished, the minister went to the lectern to read the Scripture. He stood, unable to speak. An active hush hung over the congregation, indicating a deep moving of the Spirit.

This experience brings to mind the dedication of Solomon's temple:

> It came even to pass, as the trumpeters and singers were as one, to make one sound to be heard in praising and thanking the Lord: and when they lifted up their voice with the trumpets and cymbals and instruments of musick, and praised the Lord, saying, For he is good: for his mercy endureth for ever; that then the house was filled with a cloud, even the house of the Lord; so that the priests could not stand to minister by reason of the cloud: for the glory of the Lord had filled the house of God (II Chron. 5:13–14).

These and many other experiences continually remind us that the art of music can be a powerful tool in the hands of the user. We often err by underestimating its potential for good as well as for ill.

It is evident that since man is a psychological being, and since music has this great potential to influence emotions and thoughts, the Christian should think critically about how he uses his music. It is an awesome responsibility to use this God-given tool with care and discretion.

Biblical

King David recognized the power of music and understood its message and mission as a gift from God. In his personal life David used music for praise and thanksgiving to God. When his soul was in anguish, David used music as a vehicle to soothe his broken spirit. David also ordained music to be used in religious ceremonies. In II Chronicles 29:27 we read, "And the Levites stood with the instruments of David, and the priests with the trumpets. And Hezekiah commanded to offer the burnt offering upon the altar. And when the burnt offering began, the song of the Lord began also with the trumpets, and with the instruments ordained by David king of Israel." Ezra 3:10 states: "And when the builders laid the foundation on the temple of the Lord, they set the priests in their apparel with trumpets, and the Levites the sons of Asaph with cymbals, to praise the Lord, after the ordinance of David king of Israel." For David, music spoke as the oracle of God, both in worship and in daily life.

If we miss the message and mission of church music, it may be that we have thought of music primarily as a utilitarian tool and neglect to recognize it also as an artistic tool. We see God as the creator but not as an artist. We need only turn to Genesis and read the creation story to note that when God looked upon His handiwork He saw that it was "very good." His artistic intent is revealed as "out of the ground made the Lord God to grow every tree that is pleasant to the sight and good for food" (Genesis 2:9). This is an example of a perfect blend of artistry and utility. In addition to the beauty of sight, God surely created the beauty of sound. Undoubtedly the singing of birds, the babbling of brooks, the rustling of leaves and the glorious sounds of nature all combine in a symphony of praise to God.

It should be noted that when the Lord placed man in this beautiful garden, He commanded him "to dress it and to keep it." God placed upon the first family the discipline of stewardship. Having approved the use of artistic tools in Christian expression, God also has placed within our responsibility the stewardship of church music. In keeping with the same principle, He commands us to develop it and to use it.

Martin Luther said, "When man's natural musical ability is whetted and polished to the extent that it becomes an art, then do we note with much surprise the great and perfect wisdom of God in music, which is, after all, His

9

product and His gift." The extent of our commitment to accept this stewardship challenge depends upon our honest understanding of this commandment coupled with a sincere yielding to Christian discipleship and service.

In one sense the message and mission of church music are inseparable. Music with a Christian message immediately has a mission. "Music" becomes "church music" when it is a part of God's revelation to man. It speaks of God—His nature, His power, His work, His relationship to man. It also speaks of man—his nature, his desire, his longing, his life, his relationship to man and his relationship to God. On the wings of church music is borne the inspired message from Holy Scripture. The working of the Spirit of God in the lives of men also is expressed in song. Ultimate spiritual truth in all of its aspects must characterize the true message of church music.

The mission of church music is seen more clearly in recognizing that music is a type of language that serves as a means of communicating meaning. In Deuteronomy 31:19, the Lord told Moses to write a song and teach it to the children of Israel. It was to be a witness for Him against them, because they would forget the Lord and follow their own gods. The mission of this song thus became a testimony and witness.

The Psalms also include many songs that give praise and adoration to God. The New Testament gives additional commandments to teach Christian principles through music (Eph. 5:19; Col. 3:16). Church music thus becomes a tool to assist those who have been chosen of the Lord to be apostles, prophets, evangelists, pastors and the teachers, and even choir directors, "for the perfecting of the saints, for the work of the ministry, for the edifying of the body of Christ."

This analysis of the message and mission of church music is of necessity brief and general, and does not intend to be exhaustive. These are basic tenets, intended to help in the achievement of a balance between artistic skills and spiritual communication. Proper balance includes keeping ourselves informed about the technical aspects of choral and instrumental conducting, choir organization, vocal and keyboard mastery, repertoire, and other musical disciplines. At the same time, we must grow in our desire to communicate spiritual meaning with this musical technique.

Many have observed choir directors who emphasize flawless musical performance without concern for message. On the other hand, there are choir directors who verbalize pious words and saintly phrases but who fail to recognize that, for clear communication, religious sentiment should be couched in the best possible artistic expression. In the Old Testament, God's people were commanded to give their best as a sacrifice to Him. This meant giving the firstfruits of the harvest. It would greatly enhance our relationship to God if in truth we would offer Him our best as a sacrifice of praise in song.

God's gift to the world in Jesus Christ was a perfect gift. In theological terms it can be said that excellence is an attribute of God. His Son, His plan of redemption, His creation, His love, all presented to us in perfection, demand our most excellent response.

Churches often neglect to encourage one another to give the firstfruits of their musical offering. Generally it is owing to a lack of challenge to reach for God's standard. Consciences are not pricked in settling for less than the best. It is an act of blindness to fail to heed such Scriptures as "Sing unto Him a new song; play skillfully with a loud noise." Bruce Leafblad articulates the issue convincingly:

> In the Church we are far too often willing to offer mediocre sacrifices of praise and worship, and it is a poor reflection on our Master, our theology, and our standards. Because of what the Church is and what it stands for, there is no justifiable basis for anything less than excellence in our music ministry. This plays a major part in integrity and credibility, and it causes the congregation to take us more seriously.[6]

When David spoke to the chief of the Levites to appoint their church musicians, Chenaniah was chosen because "he

---

[6]Bruce Leafblad, *The Spiritual Dimensions of Music in the Church.* (Burbank, Calif.: Manna Music, Inc., 1975), p. 3.

instructed about the song, because he was skillful" (I Chron. 15:22). On another occasion Saul sent for David because he was a "cunning player on the harp". This two-pronged approach—skillful artistry and spiritual warmth—needs to be emphasized again and again. Together they present a powerful tool for Christian expression.

Because of its powerful nature, music has been both a bane and a blessing to the church. Where the principle "to dress it and to keep it" has been observed, music has blessed. When seeking to awaken an interest and appreciation for music among the church members, the church musician should remember that they often do not have a background in music upon which to draw and are unable to share his musical idealism. They must be educated patiently and gradually exposed to what music has to offer as a means of Christian expression.

Where music has been a bane, the problems usually have stemmed from both the performer and the listener. When the Lord wants to speak through music, He often faces closed minds and hearts. Everyone, whether performing or listening, should rethink his own attitudes toward church music in order to take a balanced view and let it minister in both an artistic and utilitarian manner.

II

Common Sense in Church Music

Life has a way of bringing both security and insecurity, faith and doubt, meaning and confusion, energy and weariness. It seems as though everything good has within itself the seeds of its own destruction, or at least its own survival problems. Where food is abundant, obesity and heart trouble pose problems. A nation becomes wealthy and then experiences moral decay. High-speed transportation systems are developed, but more people are killed in accidents. Products that make life easier are manufactured, but air and water pollution confront us. A businessman works his way up to the presidency of a company, but he neglects his wife and children. A superb performing church choir is developed, but the lives of the choir members are often neglected spiritually.

Though these consequences do not necessarily follow the indicated conditions, they often do to some degree. This is an operating principle that speaks to every area of life, work, and worship. And in our consideration of church music, this principle thus points toward our involvement in interpersonal and social relationships.

It would be easy to choose music arbitrarily for its own sake or satisfy the tastes of the congregation or the choir director. Developing an awareness for avoiding such extremes is not done easily as I have learned during my own experience. From the time I directed my first church choir, which consisted of six women and one man, until I became a full-time minister of music in a large metropolitan church, my duties have been varied. In addition to completing my doctoral studies during that time, I conducted various church-music conferences and choral clinics, and taught courses in church music. Yet I had not attained full contentment from this measure of success. Rather, the ambitious drive of my twenties leaned toward a tension-filled, status-oriented program of church music. I realized that in spite of problems, the church-music programs with which I was working were growing. However, an uneasy feeling gnawed at my soul—an uneasiness that ate away at the very heart of my philosophy of church music.

Questions on my mind were: (1) Are our church-music practices relevant to the changing needs of a contemporary world? (2) Is the current probe into evangelical theology reflected in our church music? (3) Do we communicate musically with our questioning young people? (4) Do we continue to meet the spiritual needs of the older generation as we experiment with the new sounds of today? (5) In plain words, are we communicating musically the whole gospel to all people in this day of rapid change?

With these questions in mind, some of the trends, programs, and issues of church music perspective need to be explored.

Church Organization and Structure

Some persons say that the organized church has lost its momentum and usefulness. Currently some youths and skeptical adults are questioning the established church. On one side is a movement that emphasizes small group fellowships. Some Bible scholars and pastors say that group meetings of small cells may be a more realistic "assembling of the saints". Could it be that we may return to the practice of the Reformation Anabaptists in which small groups met for Bible study in private homes?

On the other hand, ecumenism is trying to break down the barriers among Christians. The first approach may lead to a cloistered, self-centered, self-righteous, noncooperative, artless entity; however, the latter approach could develop superchurches that hand down dogmas and develop elatorate organizations, without allowing the small-group experience to give the vitality and strength of deep personal interaction.

The major denominations have elaborate organizations within the church structure. These are committed to missions, evangelism, Christian education, visitation, welfare, publications, and music programs. Consequently, within the music realm, church-music conferences, choral clinics, church-music publications, and graded choir programs have become desirable as working tools of the church. Each one of us has greatly benefited from the work of the many who have contributed to such organizations.

If, however, our pattern of worship and church organization should change, the church choir of today could be known only as a fact of church history. The parishioner of tomorrow may say, "Its order of worship was beautiful; its pattern contained many historical items of interest, but it did not do what it was supposed to do."

The possibility of radical change in the organization of the church does not seem imminent, but it may not be as remote as we think. If the Sunday-morning order of worship were to change completely, how would we fit into the changing concept and practice? Would we be prepared to communicate with music if a radical structure change should come? Few answers are currently available. Much thinking and progressive planning must be done by church musicians to bring about proper guidance instead of mere reaction to the immediate pressures of events.

A meaningful change can come only when we understand the past, assess the present, and plan the future. We can best move along with change by fighting neither the past nor the future. In the shape of things to come, church music will not dictate church organization or structure. But it will remain a tool for the church to use to accomplish its work. Common sense says we must continue to win the young and strengthen the old by critically absorbing new ideas and refining the old methods and practices.

Repertoire

One of the most perplexing tensions of church music experience is the matter of music repertoire. The questions church musicians ask about repertoire are: "What should the choir sing in the morning worship service—hymns, gospel songs, anthems, or compromise with a hymn-anthem?" "Should contemporary 'pop' styles be used?" "Can accompanying instruments such as guitars and drums be used effectively?" "Will congregations sing and listen to new songs?" "Are taped accompaniments appropriate?"

Church musicians tell their people, their choirs, and their pastors that their main interest is to feed the congregation spiritual food. Nevertheless, to some extent personal ambitions, images, and tastes dictate much of the repertoire a musician chooses. Self-images are often more important than the needs of other people.

The dilemma of a choir director is not always understood nor apparent. As a university graduate student with a tender self-image, I found myself dubbed "gospel song boy" at school, while my church often viewed me as a long-haired musician (in the classical sense). The same general tension existed for me as a college choir director. Some of my colleagues in the choral conducting field made comments about my church concert repertoire such as "You have too much light music." At the same time, others complained, "Much of your music was over my head." To survive this kind of tension, a satisfying philosophy of approach and goals had to be developed.

Church-music repertoire becomes many things to many people. A partial solution is to use variety. Common sense dictates that people want music that is meaningful but also beautiful. Music, therefore, should be functionally appropriate and understood by most of the congregation. It should include a variety of forms and styles, regardless of personal preferences of the music director. The church musician, however, cannot forget that he is also a teacher and that he must help his congregation to understand and to appreciate a continually growing spectrum of church music.

Musical Taste

One of the perplexing problems in church music today is the diversity found among worshipers regarding musical tastes. Somewhat as in politics, each person feels himself to be an authority in matters of musical taste irrespective of the amount of musical training or exposure he may have had. Regardless of prior associations with a style of music, no exposure or lack of detailed and thorough study of a style of music, people seem to develop strong feelings about the music they hear. This is not new, for the church has always dealt with this situation. The difficulty of handling the problem, however, has become increasingly more acute from century to century because of the faster pace at which musical styles change. Since communication is so rapid in the twentieth century, musical styles change so fast that a person's emotional understanding and appreciation of them becomes confused, resulting in a tremendous variety of music-appreciation levels within a worshiping body.

It seems that television, radio, and the recording industry are the major musical taste setters in our society. Because boundless time is spent in listening to radio, especially by young people, the disc jockeys set the taste levels for even the Christian community. Thus the market-place type of secular music indirectly dictates what our church music is to be. Even the rapidly increasing number of Christian radio stations espouse an almost complete pop-gospel music diet. Rarely do they play excerpts of oratorios, cantatas, or anthems. This is so because of the society that has been conditioned to prefer pop music, and because station managers, announcers, and engineers generally have not had a broad music training while in school. Just as a teacher cannot teach what he does not know, a disc jockey will not play what he does not know or like.

Regarding taste levels the question is not entirely whether the music is "bad" or "good," because these judgments are difficult to define. It also includes matters of appropriateness, motivation, message, performance quality, and many other factors. A rigid authoritarian approach is not feasible since it usually is too limiting for today's broad taste levels. Robert Stevenson probes this area with the following questions.

By what criteria shall the greatness of a musical composer be measured? By the number of copies his music has sold? By the amount of recognition he received from important personages during his own lifetime? By the stir his comings and goings made in newspapers? And by what standards, more especially, shall we measure the greatness of a composer in the sacred field? Shall his worth be measured in such terms as numbers of persons added to church membership rolls, or have responded to altar calls, or have visited inquiry rooms under the influence of his music?[1]

If a broader taste level is to be developed, it is important to understand that good taste is acquired and not inherited. C. E. M. Joad, a British philosopher, states, "good taste grows slowly, through the effort to understand what is beyond us, to appreciate what we cannot yet understand. It depends on our willingness to be bored with what is good, in order that we may become bored with what is bad and so demand something better."[2] There is something to be said for Christian music in its need for stability. Some of it should serve its immediate function and then be forgotten. But some should have enduring qualities that serve for many generations, provided a means of exposure is provided. Popular music is temporal and fast-changing. Sydney J. Harris provides an interesting analysis of this phenomenon:

> Popular music changes every few weeks because it is not satisfying; its shallowness soon annoys us. Popular novels must be produced in bulk, because none of them give enough pleasure to last more than one reading. They provide sensation, no nutrition; which is why we call them sensational.
>
> Bad taste is always changing, because it cannot stand itself. Those who follow their personal preferences soon find they have no preferences except for getting rid of their old ones and finding new ones equally unsatisfying.[3]

[1]Robert M. Stevensen, *Patterns of Protestant Church Music* (Durham, N.C.: Duke University Press, 1953), p. 151.

[2]Quoted by Sidney J. Harris, "Good Taste Acquired, Not Instinctive Trait," *Tulsa Daily World,* October 4, 1976, Section A, p. 16.

[3]Ibid.

Joad's observation is that good taste "must be approached by a process of trial and error, a willingness to learn, and the humility which is prepared to accept on faith and the judgment of others what it cannot yet dare to reject on its own."[4]

The common-sense approach means being balanced in our learning, listening, and performing. Exposure to various styles of music must be broad. Donald P. Ellsworth provides a worthy insight:

> In church music which includes evangelism, musical barriers must not be constructed between the common man and the intellectual. The music of witness, just as a piece of furniture, may be completely functional even though to some it is aesthetically offensive. An artistic wedge must not be driven between those who love Renaissance anthems and those who prefer sacred folk music.[5]

Music Education—Our Responsibility?

Music educators throughout the United States are becoming increasingly alarmed that music is being squeezed out of, or is nonexistent in, the curriculum of many public schools. Emphasis upon the sciences, with a corresponding de-emphasis on the humanities, and especially the fine arts, may force the church to take more responsibility in the areas of music education. There was a day in the history of the church when most music that was taught was done as a part of the extension arm of the church.

Recent changes made by some of the state legislatures and local school boards have forced many elementary schools to eliminate all music teachers from their teaching staff. We need to recognize that in the future the church again may need to assume the leadership role in music training so that its constituents may continue to understand the role of music as a functional part of worship.

[4]Ibid.
[5]Donald Paul Ellsworth, *Christian Music In Contemporary Witness*, (Grand Rapids, Mich.: Baker Book House, 1979), p. 194.

After having spent eight years working in southern California churches with broad spending budgets, I found it an adjustment to begin working in a midwestern church with a very conservative music allotment. No one questioned the use of money to buy Sunday-school materials, but there was hesitation to provide adequate money to purchase music for the various choirs and for some church-music-staff salaries.

The reason for this may be that for a long time the work of directing a church choir or playing the organ was an unpaid position. Even today there is something which makes us recoil from the idea of paying a person for Christian service. Generally a church congregation finds it much easier to pay for "things" than for "services." Since we live in a society that operates on a monetary system, there is no way to escape the use of money as a means of carrying on the music ministry of the church.

The desire for effective music in worship demands trained persons in leadership positions. Few persons realize the energy drain, the time expended, the cost of training, and the purchase of music materials a choir director and organist encounter in their work.

It is most proper that churches continue to evaluate their stewardship practices. Perhaps continuing demands from the many church-related programs will cause church musicians to take a new look at their expenditures. But, though a proper stewardship of church money is important, the major concern in music ministry must be to have the right kind of person as choir director or organist. It is of primary importance to ask if the work to which he is assigned is being accomplished. If the Lord's work prospers, then the money issue is of secondary importance even if the music budget seems expensive.

Competition for Time

The paradox of this age is that there has never been a civilization with so many labor-saving devices, yet with so many people living frantic, activity-filled lives. And the demands upon time are increasing constantly. The Christian who honestly desires to lend his talent and energy to the work of the church, often arrives at a point of frustration because of the excessive demands put upon his time. His Christian service becomes a burden, not a joy.

There may come a time when complete reevaluation of church activity will be demanded and a review of the total Christian education, visitation, extension, and music will be necessary. What alternatives do we have? Is church music spiritually significant and vital enough to ask people to sacrifice their tightly budgeted time? It is obvious that time is one of our most precious commodities. Every Christian, then, must find the balanced approach in setting up time priorities so that all significant ministries in the church can flourish. A constant assessment of music programs is necessary so that full value is received for the time spent on it.

Church Sanctuary Acoustics[6]

A church building provides a place as well as an environment of worship. Even though Jesus speaks little about buildings, He did emphasize the need for believers to worship together. Concerning the house of worship Kliewer states:

> The church building not only houses the body of Christ in worship, it also shapes and inspires some of the most profound activities of the body of Christ. The impressions born in this place mold the feelings and convictions to the third and fourth generations. Our church buildings are a strong witness to our children and to the community regarding the nature of our faith and we should seriously question whether the places in which we meet reflect the spirit of Jesus' teaching and the nature of our church.[7]

[6]For further reading on this subject see Robert H. Mitchell, *Ministry and Music* (Philadelphia: The Westminister Press, 1978), Chapter 7, "Acoustics and Worship", pp. 114–126.

[7]Jonah C. Kliewer, "Our Buildings and Our Faith," *Christian Leader*, October 1979.

Acoustics is one of the important elements of good church-sanctuary design because the spoken word must be easily heard and the music fully experienced.

The progressive church architecture of the twentieth century brought with it a serious problem for church music. The live acoustical properties found in pretwentieth century buildings have been replaced with acoustically dead, nonreverberating materials. The stonework of city cathedrals and the hard plastered walls of small country churches have been supplanted by acoustical tile, carpeted floors, cushioned seats, and curtained backdrops. Once congregations and choirs sang with ease and natural amplification; now they hesitate to sing because they feel as if they are singing alone and miss the sound support around them. The organ sounds anemic. Choir membership suffers because the joy of blending voices is gone.

The cumulative effects of too-dead acoustics in contemporary sanctuaries are a major problem. The negative result of dead acoustical design has adversely affected the spiritual ministry of church music more than any other single cause in this century. Many congregations have expected the church music program to get a new lift by moving into a new sanctuary, and they have experienced the opposite result.

In the eighteen years I have toured with college choirs and directed choral festivals, I have conducted concerts in scores of church sanctuaries. No more than 5 to 10 percent of these had adequate acoustics for both singing and speaking. After singing in an acoustically dead church one night, one college choir member remarked, "It seems the Lord didn't speak tonight." My response was, "If the Lord didn't speak, He didn't speak to the architect." Apparently, most architects and acoustical engineers in this century have not understood the function and acoustical needs of church music. The attempt to substitute natural amplification with electronic amplification has not been successful as far as choir and congregational singing is concerned. My advice is to build a place of worship with live acoustical properties. If, after using the sanctuary awhile, the congregation determines there is too much sound reverberation or bothersome echo, acoustical material easily can be applied to soften sound reflection. On the other hand, if a sanctuary is built acoustically dead, most congregations will not be willing to tear up the ceiling or walls or pull up carpeting to replace it with material having a harder reflective surface.

My hope is that common sense will lead congregations to build new houses of worship with adequate attention to the acoustical needs of music as well as to the requirements for speaking, visual esthetics, and symbolism.

Copyright Laws[8]

When President Gerald R. Ford on October 19, 1976, signed Public Law 94-553 (the nation's first comprehensive revision of our copyright law since 1909), a new awareness of the rights of copyright holders began to emerge. By the time the law became effective on January 1, 1978, widespread abuse of the copyright law had been uncovered in churches, schools, and other organizations. The problem has become acute in recent years because photocopying machines make duplicating music so easy and inexpensive that many choir directors were simply purchasing one copy of music and duplicating multicopies at a much lower cost. Every time a piece of copyrighted music was illegally duplicated the composer/arranger, author, and publisher were robbed of their rightful compensation.

It's mystifying that even today such illegal practices are so consentingly tolerated while at the same time churches are very scrupulous about paying for utilities, Sunday-school materials, and the pastor's or custodian's services. They try to rationalize their illegal actions with such arguments as "the church is a nonprofit organization," "I'm not going to sell it," "the church doesn't give me enough money for music," or "this is for the Lord's work." None of these excuses would hold up in a court of law. Of much graver import is the tarnished reputation of witness a church may receive by breaking the law when on the contrary it should

[8]The major portion of this section was taken from the author's article "Singing To A Stolen Tune," *Christianity Today*, Vol. XXIV, No. 12, June 27, 1980, p. 11. For a more comprehensive treatment of this subject see the author's article "Piracy in the Choir Loft," *Christian Leader*, Vol. 43, No. 14, July 15, 1980.

work, worship, and conduct its business impeccably. The penalties for infringements can be severe.

A music work is copyrighted if on the title page or the first page of music is printed the word "Copyright" or the symbol ©. Additionally, the first year of publication and name of copyright owner are printed. Under the old law, the term of copyright was 28 years with possible renewal of an additional 28 years. Currently, works copyrighted prior to January 1, 1978, if renewed, will be protected for 75 years from the date the copyright was originally secured. Works copyrighted after January 1, 1978, will be protected for the life of the composer/author plus 50 years. Copyrighted music upon expiration becomes a part of the public domain. It should be noted that even out-of-print copyrighted music is protected.

Some exceptions to the exclusive rights of copyright owners have been provided under the title, "Fair Use." Many of these relate to educational uses. For the church musician, emergency copying is permitted to replace purchased copies that for any reason are not available for an imminent performance provided that in a reasonable length of time replacement copies will be purchased. The heart of the issue is that copying for the purpose of performance or for the purpose of substituting for the purchase of music is prohibited. Thus, copying to avoid the purchase of music in any way is illegal.

Pastors and musicians need to be aware that words as well as music may be copyrighted. Some churches regularly print in their worship bulletins words of contemporary gospel hymns for congregational singing purposes. This is illegal without permission of the copyright owner. A glaring abuse is the practice of printing booklets of words of contemporary gospel songs erroneously feeling that since the music is not printed the practice is legal. Furthermore, it is illegal to photograph or reproduce without permission a copyrighted work by any method including film slides and overhead projectors.

Most publishers recognize the problem that honoring the copyright law poses for the local church. Consequently, permission to reprint a hymn for a specific service is generally granted by copyright proprietors for a small fee. Blanket reprint licenses are also now available in some instances. Whenever the question arises, write to the copyright owner. You may be surprised how easy it is to be legal!

Payment for music performance is not required for services at a place of worship or other religious assembly. This includes performances of sacred music that might be regarded as "dramatic" in nature such as oratorios, cantatas, musical settings of the mass, choral services, and similar music productions provided there are no admission charges and they do not offer a commercial advantage or personal gain as described in the law. Exemption of payment does not apply to religious broadcasts from a place of worship to the public at large. Additionally, permission of the copyright owner must be obtained to make copies of a recorded performance for distribution.

The end result of illegal photocopying of music is that copyright holders lose money, the cost of music escalates to help compensate for losses, good people become cheaters, creativity is stifled, and Christian ministries become blemished. In fact, everybody loses except the manufacturers of copying machines and supplies. Common sense leads us to honor compliance with the laws of the land; however, our highest principles of obedience are derived from the laws of God. Therefore, consider the precepts expressed in the following scriptures:

"Ye shall not steal, neither deal falsely" (Leviticus 19:11).

"Thou shalt not defraud thy neighbor, neither rob him" (Leviticus 19:13).

"Withhold not good from them to whom it is due, when it is in the power of thine hand to do it" (Proverbs 3:27).

"Let your light so shine before men, that they may see your good works, and glorify your Father which is in heaven" (Matthew 5:16).

Nonverbal Communication

Early in my choir-conducting experience I learned that the effectiveness of my choir ministry depended upon many nonmusical factors such as the appearance of the choir, facial expression, attitude, and stage conduct. It soon became apparent that this nonverbal communication could greatly enhance or inhibit the effectiveness of a performance.

A mood abroad today tends to ignore this principle. Our emphasis on individual expression and "do your own thing" makes collective endeavors much more complicated. This difficulty of achieving unified action often results in conflicting signals given by verbal and nonverbal expressions.

Why do these problems arise? First, we fail to recognize that the meanings of nonverbal symbols change over a period of time. And second, the rate of understanding these changes varies greatly. For example, in the late 1960's beards and long hair on men brought tension into many adult church-choir programs. One may regard this as a trivial item with which to be concerned. That is true, except for the powerful aspects of nonverbal communication. The beard and the long hair had become symbols of drug use, immorality, and disregard for personal cleanliness. Because of these associations, many parishioners saw the long-haired choir member singing gospel words while his appearance was saying something unchristian.

How do we reconcile the two means of expression? In the first place, we need to recognize that both verbal and nonverbal means of communication are operative. We do not communicate in segments. We declare ourselves as total beings.

In the second place, we need to understand what a symbol is saying to the viewer. For example, the swastika, a form of Greek cross in early Christian times, became an infamous symbol for the German Nazi regime. It would have been foolish for an American to wear the swastika on his lapel during World War II and tell people he was wearing a symbol of the cross. The message of the swastika during those years was such a powerful symbol for Nazism that it could never communicate the message of the cross. Citing a more common example, many Christians are very careful about the language they use, yet their appearance communicates a language that may be quite obscene. Little comfort can be gained from the excuse that people should look upon the inner man, not his outside appearance. Possibly more is said about the inner man by his outside appearance and actions than we would like to admit. Much truth rides in the cliché that actions speak louder than words.

Albert Mehrabian states, "in the realm of feelings, our facial expressions, postures, movements, and gestures are so important that when our words contradict the silent messages contained within them, others mistrust what we say— they rely almost completely on what we do."[9] Illustrating the differential impact of verbal, vocal, and facial cues Mehrabian devised a formula for communication as 7% (verbal), 38% (vocal) and 55% (facial). Obviously, most music leaders are not aware of this nonverbal dimension of communication. Greater sensitivity to all communication factors needs to be developed.

Third, common sense dictates that in public performance we need to strive for moderation in appearance so that the nonverbal communication will not obscure the verbal message. Naturally, it is necessary to shift with the styles. The beard and long hair have begun to lose their symbolic association and once again have become more acceptable. Time is a great neutralizer. Nevertheless, we need to seek the middle ground in style and call attention to the message we sing rather than to our grooming tastes.

Fourth, nonverbal communication has the potential of being a positive adjunct to musical performance. We need to blend the visual message with the auditory. Hamlet aptly said, "Suit the action to the word, the word to the action." Effective communication in a subculture or a foreign culture demands the adoption of some of its life-styles. Cultural anthropologists know that a negative symbol in one culture may be positive in another. Therefore, decide whom you want to speak to, get to know his life-style, then speak his language verbally and nonverbally in a complementary way.

[9]Albert Mehrabian, *Silent Messages* (Belmont, Calif.: Wadsworth Publishing Co., 1971). p. iii.

Finally, here are three guidelines for applying our musical principles. Following these in the light of the Word of God will help to improve church music practices.

Clarify Goals and Objectives

If your goals are not clearly defined, the shifting sands of our times will lead you off course. Our problem too often is that our goals are vague and often selfish rather than God-centered. The clearest manifestation of this is seen as we choose our music repertoire. It is only natural for us to want people to like our selections of music. However, if we cannot effectively use our favorite music style such as a pop folk hymn or a sixteenth-century motet, we should not feel that our goals have been undermined.

It is important to realize that the decision of repertoire is linked decidedly with a functional point of view. We should ask, even though it is an oversimplification, "Does this music communicate to the people for whom I am singing or playing?" People do not come to a worship service or a Bible class to have a class on music appreciation. They come to encounter the Lord. And our music must have the objective of being the catalyst that will spark a light of Christian purpose and motivation. If a folk hymn does it, we should be open to its use. If a Bach cantata does it, we must learn to perform this music with feeling. This approach, of necessity, includes the objective of broadening the congregation's musical horizons so that their potential for experiencing an increased spectrum of music is enlarged.

It could be that in the future a jazz combo will become an accepted part of our music experience in the worship service. Note the musical changes that have occurred in church history. Styles have varied from Gregorian chants, motets, chorales, and psalm tunes to hymns, Negro spirituals, and gospel songs and choruses. Music styles, techniques, and forms have changed throughout the centuries, but the gospel they communicated has not changed.

We must always keep ultimate goals and objectives clear, but we cannot afford in a changing world to hang our hat on one music style and feel confident that we are communicating the whole gospel to the whole person. The gospel is the message, and the music is the vehicle of communication. The vehicle changes, not the message. In church music, we cannot assume that our objective is "art for art's sake." Instead it must clearly be "art for Christ's sake."

Approach New Ideas With An Open Mind

This may be the biggest hurdle most of us have to face. The reason is that through years of exposure to various types of church music, we have developed our personal likes and dislikes. But we must recognize that some of the music we thought could not serve spiritually may be exactly what is needed. For instance, I hardly know how to evaluate today's pop and rock idiom. In the first place, we live too close to the time of its development, and we know too little about its effect to make final, valid judgments. I still recoil from the idea of jazz and rock as an effective worship tool. Nevertheless, as a twentieth-century being, living with twentieth-century people, I must communicate to a twentieth-century society. Each person of the twentieth-century needs to be brought the saving message of Jesus Christ, and you and I must do it even if it means using the contemporary popular music idioms.

If, on the other hand, our minds are closed to the use and appreciation of older music such as Handel's "Messiah" (composed during the baroque period), we are just as derelict as those who do not accept the new styles. It is natural to feel more comfortable with the familiar. I often hear someone say, "I know what I like." But in reality he is saying, "I like what I know."

We must encourage one another to be more pliable in perspective and more willing to enlarge our choices of music with an ear to the needs and tastes of our audience.

Take a Balanced View

No matter what position you may take, someone will take an opposite view. One person likes chamber music,

29

the next is a Beethoven fan, another wants Gregorian chants, and still another opts for religious pop. As you guide your ship of church music through a stormy sea of change, may you not ride on only one wave! We communicate with the greatest number of people if we keep a balanced repertoire before them, and the repertoire must give each person the opportunity to experience something spiritual for the immediate present. It must also give him something new to grow on.

III

Spiritual Music For a Spiritual Church

Regardless of its form, style, or medium, all honest church music should communicate spiritual truth. But what is meant by spiritual music?

Scripture helps us by urging, "Let the word of Christ dwell in you richly in all wisdom; teaching and admonishing one another in psalms and hymns and spiritual songs, singing with grace in your hearts to the Lord" (Col. 3:16; see also Eph. 5:18–19).

Is music to be judged "spiritual" only when it contains the name of God, when it follows a set pattern of stanza and chorus, when its rhythm fits a certain mood, or when it is accepted by some church group? These all present valid considerations, but each alone falls short of defining the true essence of "spiritual music for a spiritual church."

Most music has melody, rhythm, harmony, form, and texture, but these characteristics in themselves are neither spiritual nor nonspiritual. The worth or meaning of music is determined only by the combination of these musical elements and upon its use or function.

Music can be a blessing or a curse, spiritual or unspiritual, depending upon how it is used. This tool of music makes its impression like a movie camera, as it reveals the hidden secrets of God's creation or flaunts the lust of Hollywood. It can be like an automobile that serves as a necessary means of transportation or as a tool to kill. Explosives make new roads or bomb a city. Alcohol can keep a car radiator from freezing or dull the senses of a human body as it flows through the blood stream. So too with music. It can edify or destroy.

If we speak of spiritual music, we must talk about spiritual men and women who use music for spiritual ends. To have spiritual music, there must be a spiritual church. For a spiritual church to grow, it must have spiritual music.

31

Dr. Donald Hustad, in a speech at the National Church Music Fellowship Convention in Chicago, said that for music to have a spiritual meaning, it must pass through three doors.

The first door is the senses. Any impression that comes to a person, whether by word or by song, must come first through the door of the senses. However, much of the music we hear never goes much farther than this first door. Perhaps this is not all bad. We need music that is entertaining and relaxing. Children need good, clean, fun songs in order to develop positive, wholesome attitudes toward music. Unfortunately, much of this music merely tickles the senses and allows little room for spiritual enrichment. Many have interpreted "peppy" music as being the major criterion for a spirit-filled song. It is true that in many cases, joyful music has a fast tempo and dotted rhythms, but these are not the main ingredients of spiritual music. For deeper, spiritual experiences, music needs to travel through other doors.

The second door is the mind. We hear music with our ears, but we must also grasp its spiritual truth and its intellectual significance. In order for us to respond intelligently to a spiritual impulse, music must have meaning. Consequently, all the sensations of music—the words of the hymn, the atmosphere created by the organ prelude, the text of the anthem—must be understood before they can achieve their spiritual results.

Music heard at this level is valuable as wholesome entertainment and pleasure. It provides mental therapy and expands the mind. It is almost universally acknowledged that Beethoven, Brahms, and Bach offer more than pure enjoyment. They help meet deeper human needs.

There are, however, various reasons why we find certain kinds of music difficult to pass through this second door. First, the music may be too complex for the person to comprehend. Second, the music may be "cheap"; its appeal may be only to the senses and may not reach the intellect. Music of this kind often overstresses rhythm and dynamics, neglecting other fine elements of music. Music that appeals mainly to the feet often has little appeal to the mind. When music passes through door number two, it affords the opportunity for intellectual exercise and growth. Even here, however, it does not guarantee a spirit-filled experience.

The third door is the door of the heart. This door can be unlocked only from the inside and must be opened by the Holy Spirit. In this chamber, music is translated into spiritual meaning as it leads one to praise, prayer, confession, and commitment. The Word of God printed on the page becomes a part of the spirit of man. Written music and words also become, so to speak, flesh and blood.

The Contents of Spiritual Music

Since music is able to identify with all human expressions, it is possible to influence and, to some degree, to teach Christian principles through music. Following are some of the more obvious Christian tenets that music can undergird through a teaching program.

Salvation

Since the days of the revivals of John and Charles Wesley and Dwight L. Moody, the gospel song, directing the sinner's attention to his lost condition, has had a useful position in church music. Throughout the total history of the church, however, music has been one of the voices for the proclamation of the good news of Christ's redemption.

Note how often the psalmist cries, "Save us, O God." The New Testament admonishes us to proclaim salvation through teaching with "psalms, hymns, and spiritual songs." Prereformation Christians sang "laudi spirituali," which were "grass-root" expressions of the common people, resulting from religious revivals of the thirteenth century. Some sang these songs as they marched through the streets, scourging themselves in protest to the pleasure-ridden world and as penance for the indifference of the people to God. Out of the nineteenth-century revival movement came one of the most significant music forms ever used for evangelism, the gospel song. It is still used today to bring the message of salvation to lost sinners and invite them to make decisions for Jesus Christ.

Doctrine

Luther's great concern during the Reformation was to teach believers the fundamental doctrines of the Christian faith. Since the Bible was not readily available to the common people, he had the problem of teaching them scriptural truths and doctrines. Believing that perhaps congregational singing could be used as a teaching aid, Luther wrote to a friend:

> I am willing to make German psalms for the people, according to the example set by the prophets and ancient fathers; . . . spiritual songs [hymns] in order that the Word of God may be conserved among the people through singing also. [1]

Since development of the Lutheran hymn form, known as the "chorale", countless hymns have been written and used to teach biblical truth. Scripture songs have to this day served this function. Most hymnals have topical indexes that list hymns dealing with various aspects of the Christian faith. We thus have a heritage of hymns that reaches back to the Reformation and that can be used to help teach fundamental Bible doctrines.

Christian Living

Singing of sacred songs is not confined to the church sanctuary. It is also to be found in the home, at school, at work, and in social gatherings. Songs that give us encouragement, instruction, admonition, and challenge can be a part of our daily experience. In addition to singing of hymns, many people find blessing by using the hymnal for devotional reading.

[1]Friedrich Spitta, "Ein feste Burg ist unser Gott." Die Lieder Luthers in ihrer Bedeutung für das evangelische Kirchenlied (Göttingen: 1905), p. 9; as cited by Walter E. Buszin, "Luther on Music." Buszin's brackets.

Fellowship

One of the objectives at the beginning of a youth meeting, prayer meeting, or a worship service, is to bring together the thought, mood, and spirit of a corporate group of people. It is said that only after a group of people have sung a hymn together can they become a congregation—a unified group of believers joined together in worship and fellowship. Because we come together and focus our attention upon spiritual things through singing, we join together in fellowship. In singing, barriers are broken down, attention is more sharply focused, unity is fostered, morale is raised, and spiritual fellowship is enhanced.

Prayer

We usually experience prayer on an individual basis. However, in singing it is possible, in a unified way, for a corporate body of believers to bring their petitions, aspirations, praise, and thanksgiving to God in prayer. Most hymnals contain a section of prayer hymns.

Reverence

In today's world of feverish activity, frantic promotion and close familiarity, our respect for God often becomes routine. Too often disrespect, loudness, and a spirit of frivolity make reverence for God a mockery. We need to bow in humility before our great God. Music can help to quiet our hearts and souls so that we can more clearly recognize who our God really is. Music makes it possible for us to respond in reverence. Why should we want to reverence God? Note the following scriptures:

Ye shall keep my sabbaths, and reverence my sanctuary: I am the Lord (Lev. 19:30).

Thy way, O God, is in the sanctuary: who is so great a God as our God? (Ps. 77:13).

But the Lord is in His holy temple: let all the earth keep silence before Him (Hab. 2:20).

And he said, Draw not nigh hither: put off thy shoes from off thy feet, for the place whereon thou standest is holy ground (Ex. 3:5).

These scriptures indicate that God is holy, and that our attitude should include deep respect, holy awe, and affection for Him. Even though we no longer live under Old Testament law, it is noteworthy to recognize how much the Holy of Holies in the temple was viewed with reverence and awe. God does not change!

How can reverence be taught? In one sense reverence cannot be taught. Like mother love and the taste for good food, it must be experienced. Words help to explain, but in the end they must be experienced to be understood. It is obvious that one's surroundings can enhance the spirit of reverence. We can set up visual and auditory conditions that are conducive to the spirit of reverence. This can be done, simply because everything we see, feel, or hear, affects us. Think of the color of a room, music played or sung, lighting, or the physical actions of teacher, minister, or choir. They all affect us.

A Sunday school superintendent once complained that he had difficulty in quieting the children when they came into the assembly room. I visited his Sunday school department and noticed the pianist playing a loud and vigorous tune as the children were coming in. The loud music was stirring the children toward active and spirited expressions. The situation later improved considerably when she played softer and meditative music. Obviously the use of visual aids, music, or a combination of the arts may help us achieve an atmosphere of reverence and respect.

We should be aware, however, that reverence is not an end product but rather a by-product. The reverence that flows from the inner man comes as a result of his concept of who God is. It is a matter of theology. I am impressed with the reverence expressed in Roman Catholic churches. Their theology is especially manifested in their belief in transubstantiation, that is, that the communion wine and bread are changed into the actual blood and body of Jesus

Christ. And in their response to "seeing" Jesus Christ actually on the altar before them, they seemingly cannot help but respond with deep awe and reverence.

Protestants also say that Jesus Christ is with us in our services, but in spirit. Do we really believe it? Judging by the way we behave in our services, one would hardly believe that we are there to honor and worship the Creator of the world and the Saviour of mankind. We criticize the Catholic Church for some of its beliefs and practices. Yet we as Protestants stand open to serious indictment concerning our true beliefs and attitude toward God. True reverence is experienced when we recognize our Lord as worthy, holy, great, mighty, as well as being friend, comforter, and one who is closer than a brother.

Worship

The Christian has been commanded to worship God. He wants to worship God because he has been saved from sin through Christ's sacrifice and He is now the Lord of his life. It is in worship that music finds its greatest identification with this religious expression. In praise, adoration, confession, and dedication, music greatly enhances the worship experience. The experiences of worship through music are not limited to a certain music style, medium, or form. When the psalmist said, "Let every thing that hath breath praise the Lord," he certainly included using everything from gospel songs to chorales, Gregorian chants to psalm tunes, guitars and drums to pipe organs. Everything can be used to praise God.

Music in the Teaching of Christian Principles

It is the right and privilege of every Christian believer to use music in his Christian experience. The effective use of music in the total work of the church, however, does not come automatically. It must be nurtured and taught. This effort needs the support of both the church and the family.

Much of the child's attitude towards music and the church are developed in the home.[2] Thus, if music is to have a meaningful ministry, certain basic facts about its nurture must be observed.

Compatibility

The music used should be compatible with the text. For example, a highly rhythmic, jazzy tune does not usually lend itself to the spirit of devotional prayer. On the other hand, tunes with a slow tempo and rhythm do not support a fresh-spirited testimony. The premise is that music should appropriately clothe the text with beauty and strength, as well as undergrid its meaning. One must recognize that this type of judgment is subjective and should be tempered by the cultural background of the people using the music. A rule of thumb says that if the musical setting calls attention to itself instead of the words, it is not a good setting for the text.

Here are some good examples of the marriage of music and text:

1. "The Solid Rock": Text by Edward Mote, music by William B. Bradbury. The first four notes of the melody, set in a trumpetlike call of attention, suggest an appropriate mood for this gospel song that speaks of positive confidence and faith.
2. "When I Survey the Wondrous Cross": Text by Isaac Watts; tune, *Hamburg,* arranged by Lowell Mason.
3. "More Holiness Give Me": Text and tune by Philip P. Bliss.
4. "O God, Our Help in Ages Past": Text by Isaac Watts; tune, *St. Anne,* attributed to William Croft.
5. "More Love to Thee, O Christ": Text by Elizabeth Prentiss, tune by William H. Doane.

[2]Alfred E. Lunde, *Christian Education Thru Music* (Wheaton, Illinois: Evangelical Teacher Training Association, 1978). See chapter "Sharing Music at Home and Church (pp. 67–80)."

Now note how some texts and music are incompatible in harmony and mutual respect.

1. "Love Lifted Me": Text by James Rowe, tune by Howard E. Smith. The expression of the stanza depicts a tragic, human condition. The music set to this text, however, is rollicking and swingy. I became aware of the misleading character of this music during a young people's singspiration when someone sang, "I was sinking deep in sin—yippie!" The mood of the music overshadowed the text to such an extent that this young person lost the sense of the message and yielded to the opposing spirit of the music.

2. "Alas and Did My Saviour Bleed?": Text of the stanzas by Isaac Watts, refrain and tune by Ralph E. Hudson. The music for the stanzas of this gospel song is adequate. The problem lies in the refrain that Mr. Hudson added. The spirit of the verses is to help the singer understand the extreme pain and suffering Jesus Christ endured for our salvation. To juxtapose a spirited and jolly musical chorus between the stanzas is asking for more than most of us can emotionally understand. Either we will dwell on the spirit of the refrain or the spirit of the stanzas. A compromise might be to sing the refrain as a joyful testimony following the singing of all the contemplative stanzas.

3. "More Like the Master": Text and tune by Charles H. Gabriel. This gospel song is another example where the stanzas seem compatible with the music, but the rhythm of the refrain is too frivolous for serious decision making.

4. "Living for Jesus": Text by Thomas O. Chisholm and tune by C. Harold Lowden. This gospel song, a favorite of many, is rather tuneful and interesting. However, the tendency toward a waltz rhythm in the refrain is distracting. Its greatest problem lies in the mismatching of musical accents with the word syllables. Longer musical notes tend to give a feeling of accent, which, in this song, lead to all kinds of wrong accents of syllables. The italicized syllables in the following stanza show where the musical stress lies, and indicate the problem:

Liv-*ing* for Je-*sus* a life *that* is true
Striv-*ing* to please *Him* in all *that* I do;
Yield-*ing* al-le-*giance,* glad-heart-*ed* and free
This *is* the path-*way* of bless-*ing* for me.

I was once asked to review a film on Christian steward-ship that had been criticized for its background music. While viewing the film, I soon realized that this otherwise excellent film was suffering from music that did not rein-force the message on the screen. For example, a popular version of "Now I Belong to Jesus" was being played as a description of a materialistic Christian was given. This same tune was used as a background for a description of a South American woman living deep in superstition. When the narrator spoke about persons dying without the knowl-edge of Jesus Christ, the background music was a light, lilting arrangement that said, "I've discovered the way of gladness." When the narrator intended to bring the viewer toward a point of personal commitment, the background music was a dainty, pizzicato, orchestral version of "Jesus Loves Me." The result was an incompatibility between nar-ration and music.

People in our churches are becoming more and more sensitive to the language of music and are soon irritated when the music does not amplify the text but rather con-tradicts it.

Repetition

Repetition is an important technique in music teaching. To receive full value from singing a hymn, the music as well as the text must have meaning. Therefore, music demands comprehension before it can perform its function with the text. Of course, a text can be understood without music as well as with music. But unfamiliarity with the music often becomes a barrier to congregational singing. Often people close their hymnals when they discover an unfamiliar tune. The problem is not the text—they read English. The prob-lem is the unfamiliar tune. People will more readily sing an unfamiliar text with a familiar tune, than a familiar text with an unfamiliar tune. It seems important then, that new anthems, hymns, gospel songs, and organ preludes be repeated often enough so that the congregation will feel familiar with them.

Relevancy

Discrimination in the use of music is important so that whenever music is used in any religious service it will be appropriate and relevant to the total purpose of the service. Unfortunately, many potentially useful songs have not been used effectively because they have not been appropriately placed in a service. They were either thematically out of place with a particular program, or the style of music was not suited for the kind of program or mood intended. Once during a baptismal service, the song leader noticed he had given an incorrect hymn number. Since it was too late to change, the congregation sang "Almost Persuaded" during the baptism. The song leader later apologized to the pastor and was astonished when the pastor responded, "What was wrong?" The pastor simply showed insensitivity to the purpose of congregational singing.

Sometimes strange and humorous combinations of sermon and song titles have been listed in sequence when the pastor and music director did not plan together. One pastor's sermon, "Launch Out Into the Deep," followed the choir singing, "Pull for the Shore." The sermon, "Who Will Go for Me?" was followed by the congregation singing, "Search Me, O God." An old story tells of the preacher, who, in a sermon on temperance, stated that all sinners should take their booze and throw it into the river. The congregation was then led in singing "Shall We Gather at the River?"

I cannot vouch for the authenticity of these stories, but they do illustrate the need for careful planning of worship music to make it relate to the total service.

Such planning requires an understanding of the functions of the various forms of church music and the differences among them.

The gospel song is a religious song in which text and music are designed specifically for use in revival services and fellowship meetings.[3] However, it is now being used extensively in evangelistic churches during their worship services. The texts are usually subjective, emphasizing testimony, fellowship, and invitation. The following are some definitions given by various church musicians and theologians.

A gospel song is a testimony song... addressed to people. Phil Kerr[4]

The term "Gospel Songs" is applied to a certain class of sacred lyrics, chiefly of an evangelistic character, composed for use in popular gatherings of a heterogeneous character. D. R. Breed[5]

The words are usually simple and easily remembered and concern themselves largely with the individual's salvation. The personal pronouns "I" and "my" predominate. The tunes are rhythmic and catchy and always have a refrain added. Their harmonies are largely built on the simply tonic, dominant, and subdominant chords. The masses of the people readily learned to sing these tunes and experienced a thrill in singing them which the use of the more stately and solid hymns failed to effect. Lester Hostetler[6]

They are subjective songs emphasizing human experience and testimony. Frequently these songs press for a decision on the part of the listener. The music is normally simple, easily sung and easily learned, with simple harmony and lilting rhythm. In form it is free; in character it is emotional; in purpose and spirit it is evangelistic. The songs usually develop a single thought, which generally culminates after each verse with a chorus or refrain bringing unity to all of the stanzas. Donald P. Ellsworth[7]

[3]For a more comprehensive history of the gospel song see James Sallee, A History of Evangelistic Hymnody (Grand Rapids, Mich.: Baker Book House, 1978).

[4]Phil Kerr, Music in Evangelism (Glendale, Calif.: Gospel Music, 1939), p. 66.

[5]David R. Breed, History and Use of Hymns and Hymn Tunes (New York: Revell, 1903), p. 331.

[6]Lester Hostetler, Handbook to the Mennonite Hymnary (Newton, Kansas: Gen. Conf. Mennonite Church of North America, 1949), p. xxvii.

[7]Donald P. Ellsworth, Christian Music in Contemporary Witness (Grand Rapids, Mich.: Baker Book House, 1979), p. 93.

By contrast, the hymn, much older than the gospel song, has had its greatest use in the worship service. Consequently, it has gone through more changes and has had a broader worldwide usage. The following are some definitions of the hymn given by various church musicians and theologians.[8]

A hymn is the praise of God by singing. A hymn is a song embodying the praise of God. If there is merely praise but not praise of God it is not a hymn. For it to be a hymn, it is needful, therefore, for it to have three things—praise, praise of God, and these sung. Augustine[9]

A Christian hymn is a lyric poem, reverently and devotionally conceived, which is designed to be sung and which expresses the worshipper's attitude toward God or God's purposes in human life. It should be simple and metrical in form, genuinely emotional, poetic, and literary in style, spiritual in quality, and in its ideas so direct and so immediately apparent as to unify a congregation while singing it. Carl F. Price[10]

The present-day Protestant conception of the word "hymn" is that it is a religious poem divided into stanzas which a congregation may sing by repeating the same tune to each stanza. Robert Guy McCuthan[11]

A hymn is a sacred poem expressive of devotion, spiritual experience or religious truth, fitted to be sung by an assembly of people. Harvey B. Marks[12]

Charles Gold wrote one of the first masters' theses dealing with the subject of the gospel song. He listed the follow-

[8]For an excellent discussion of the hymn see section, "The Hymn in Perspective" dealing with the hymn as literature, music, scripture, and theology in Harry Eskew and Hugh T. McElrath, *Sing With Understanding* (Nashville, Tenn.: Broadman Press, 1980), pp. 13–71.

[9]Cited by Hostetler, p. xii.

[10]Carl F. Price, *What Is a Hymn?* Paper VI of the Hymn Society of America, 1937, p. 8.

[11]Robert Guy McCutchan, *Hymns in the Lives of Men* (New York: Abingdon-Cokesbury, 1945), p. 27.

[12]Harvey B. Marks, *Rise and Growth of English Hymnody* (New York: Revell, 1937), p. 30.

ing interesting and practical comparisons of the hymn and the gospel song.[13]

HYMN	GOSPEL SONG
1. Primary purpose is to glorify God. Both objective and subjective in character.	1. Primarily a song of exhortation, testimony, warning, persuasion. Usually subjective in character [using the pronouns "I" and "my"].
2. Used primarily in worship services.	2. Used primarily in revival meetings, evangelistic services and fellowship periods. [Used, however, in worship services in evangelistic-type churches.]
3. Music is stately, dignified and devotional in character.	3. Usually rhythmically fast. A pervasive enthusiasm.
4. Notes of even time value. Comparatively few notes of eighth or sixteenth value.	4. Notes of varied time values. Containing, at times, dotted eights and sixteenths.
5. Text is usually set to music without use of chorus or refrain technique.	5. Verse with chorus or refrain pattern predominating.

Realizing that gospel songs and hymns serve a variety of different functions, we should be sensitive in planning their use. It is not only a case of the best tune or text, but it must also be appropriate for the situation.

The Quality of Spiritual Music

It was a warm afternoon in Italy. I stood viewing the bronze doors to the baptistery of the Cathedral of Florence

[13]Charles E. Gold, "A Study of the Gospel Song" (Master's thesis, U. of S. Calif., 1953), pp. 88–89.

that Michelangelo called the "Gates of Paradise." In relief sculpture from top to bottom were pictured many of the stories I had read in the Bible.

Later, when I was told of the many years it took the artist to carve the pictures, I asked that guide why anyone would take so much out of his life to do such work.

"In those days," he replied, "few people could read. The printing process had not been developed, and the only way the Bible stories could be given to the masses was through the preacher's words. In order to help people to remember the Bible stories, many artists were motivated to paint, carve, and sculpture images depicting Bible stories and personalities. It was a simple case of using visual aids."

We need to look upon these artists in one sense as translators of the Bible. Today we have many new English translations of the Bible. The goal of each translator has been to make the Bible's meaning clearer to the reader. Thus an artist would give five to ten years of his life for the creation of one large painting or mural for a church. He knew that his artwork would speak to everyone who viewed it. Therefore, he gave extreme care, skill, and patience to his art so it would in truth, "speak" the Word of God.

I was raised in a rural church that fostered singing but generally did not use the visual arts. Early in my life I became particularly aware of the negative aspects and abuses of the symbolism of the past. I now recognize that the spoken language is also a type of symbolism, and I have come to understand the rich blessing in the use of symbols in expressing religious thought.

While serving as minister of music in the Tenth Avenue Baptist Church of Los Angeles, I became aware of this when my pastor gave a series of sermons entitled, "From Advent to Easter." The pastor took his sermon topics from the stained-glass windows that surrounded the nave. These windows depicted many of the events of the life of Jesus Christ while on earth. For months afterward, I frequently spent time meditating in the sanctuary and viewing the various windows. Many truths that the pastor had given in his sermons were again impressed upon my mind. I learned that these windows could preach if a person would only stop to look, pray, and meditate.

Musicians also have tried to speak with the same kind of dedication and sincerity as have painters and sculptors. Johann Sebastian Bach was such a man. He caught the dynamics and power of the Reformation and of the chorale that came from it. Because Christians were once again being given the opportunity to sing in worship, Bach was inspired to produce church music that has never been surpassed. On his manuscripts, Bach would put the notation, "Soli Deo Gloria" (to God alone be the glory). Whether the piece was a short keyboard composition, a cantata, an organ fugue, or a chorale prelude, Bach's composing came under this one overall motivating spirit.

Men like Bach were God-pleasers first, and only second, man-pleasers. It is humbling to realize that such great masters, who had the technique of their talent so highly refined and so well under control, still possessed an overwhelming desire to make every note, every stroke of the brush, every chip from the carving knife, count for God. They undoubtedly wrestled with the temptation of becoming men-pleasers first, but their work demonstrates their desire to please God first.

To have spiritual music there must be spiritual people. But spiritual music goes far beyond the spectrum of the music itself. Possibly church music would have greater meaning for us if we understood the lives of our richly talented brothers and sisters. We just don't seem to come into meaningful contact with the lives of those men and women—both past and present—whose lives have been deeply moved by the Spirit of God. We do not sense the passion of the painter who, hundreds of years ago, wanted to put the story of Jesus Christ on canvas. We are unaware of the devotion of the eighteenth-century musician who perceived ideas of sound, then jotted them down on paper with symbols that you and I can read today.

Are we spiritual people? We live and work in our communities in our own way, just as countless believers have done before us. We sell food in the grocery stores, we sell garments to clothe our bodies, we build houses for shelter, we stand in the classrooms as teachers, we study in the libraries as students. In all this, we, like Bach, can say with Thanksgiving, "Soli Deo Gloria." In this kind of atmosphere we can truly have spiritual music for a spiritual church.

But too often we don't realize what it is like to struggle for existence in the Third World. We don't know the pressures of the executive on Madison Avenue. We are isolated from the ghetto inhabitant. We are strangers in the "global village." Consequently, we communicate with difficulty.

When the doctor told my brother that he had only three to six months to live, he took immediate inventory of his life. The day after he and his wife arrived home from his last visit to the doctor, they asked each other (and I'm sure they asked God), "How do we face this?" They shared the mutual confidence that they would live a day at a time— live to the fullest each day—and "Soli Deo Gloria."

Too often we do not feel the urgency of the moment, and we do not ask the ultimate questions. A cantata by Bach forcefully entreats us, "Sleepers wake, the night is flying."

How can a musician work toward experiencing spiritual music? There is one primary step. Whether performer or listener, he must be committed to Jesus Christ. He must respond to Him in the spirit of "Soli Deo Gloria." As an interpreter of God's message through music, he must sing or play in the most effective manner possible. This is the way to make music communicate with beauty, power, accuracy, and meaning.

The story is told of a group of tourists in an art gallery in Europe. Upon viewing a Rembrandt masterpiece, one tourist remarked to the guide, "I don't see what's so great about that painting." The guide replied, "Sir, the painting is not on trial; you are!"

All of us must take an inward look. When music does not seem to be fulfilling its spiritual mission, the fault may be in us and not in the music. Once after a Sunday-morning service I was greatly encouraged by an elderly gentleman who said that the anthem was too complicated for him to understand. He could, however, see that it was speaking to many in the congregation, and he felt that the Lord had led the choir to sing the anthem for that particular service. He further stated that he would try to learn more of the language of music so that he, too, could respond to the spiritual ministry of such an anthem. This open attitude made further exciting spiritual experiences possible for him.

IV

The Drama of Worship

Since the beginning of the Christian Church, believers have met together regularly to worship their Lord. This joining together to worship God is the ultimate of Christian expression. The worshiping Christian is obeying the Lord's commandment and is being nurtured toward a deeper, more mature Christian life. However, true worship is not confined or limited to place or time. It can occur in private as well as in a large group.

Throughout church history, corporate worship has taken many forms and procedures. it is regrettable that in the minds of many believers, worship is something cold and distant. Many persons do not understand what is supposed to happen in a worship service. The cynic may say, "So much of our worship service is pious rigamorole, a sanctimonious melange of prayers, hymns, and Bible readings all strung together." Unfortunately, some so-called worship services fit this pattern. I believe, however, that if worship were viewed and practiced as "drama," it might take on new vigor and interest. If the service had a thread of drama woven into the fabric of the whole worship service, it would increase the spiritual intensity. In drama there is continuity, action, and a dominant theme, as well as variety, involvement, and participation. Our discussion will thus focus on helping the Christian to understand the purposes of worship and how he contributes to it.

The Worship Service

What Is Worship?

The word *worship* is ordinarily used to describe almost any type of religious service where a group of people gather. An obvious misunderstanding exists as to what a worship service should be. This often leads to irrelevant and confusing religious meetings. A diluted, purposeless worship service manages only to leave the worshiper unfulfilled and dissatisfied.

Volumes have been written to help define worship. Anne Ortland describes it as "admiring God."[1]Ralph Martin asserts, "To worship God is to ascribe to Him supreme worth, for He alone is worthy."[2] James White speaks of worship in terms of what happens: "called from the world, we come together, deliberately seeking to approach reality at its deepest level by encountering God in and through Jesus Christ and by responding to this awareness."[3] Bruce Leafblad gives a threefold definition.

First, worship is that wonderfully mysterious activity in which we *declare* to God that He is the supreme value in our lives, and at the same time we *express* that evaluation.

Second, worship is that holy and intimate activity in which we declare to God that He has our *supreme affection* in life, and having declared such, we also express that affection in active love.

Third, worship is that humbling yet compelling activity in which we declare to God that He has our *supreme commitment* in life.[4]

Paul Hoon describes worship as a "God's revelation" and "man's response" encounter. He states:

This conviction may be elaborated by variously saying that Christian worship is God's revelation of himself in Jesus Christ and man's response; that it is the dialogue between

[1]Anne Ortlund, *Up With Worship* (Glendale, Calif.: Regal Books, 1975), p. 100.

[2]Ralph P. Martin, *Worship In The Early Church* (Grand Rapids, Mich.: William B. Eerdmans Publishing Co., 1974), p. 10.

[3]James F. White, *Introduction to Christian Worship* (Abingdon Press, Nashville, Tenn., 1980), p. 21.

[4]Bruce Leafblad, *Music, Worship, and the Ministry of the Church* (Portland, Oregon, Department of Information Resource Service, Western Conservative Baptist Seminary, 1978), pp. 21-22.

man and God through the Word; that it is Christ's priestly action kindling the priestly action of the faithful; that it is the re-enactment of *Kultmysterium,* the cultic "mystery" of Christ; that it is encounter of Christ in His Real Presence with the human soul. These theological metaphors, however, are only variations of the central conviction that Christian worship is grounded in the reality of the action of God toward the human soul in Jesus Christ and in man's responsive action through Jesus Christ.[5]

In a class on music and worship, Dr. Charles C. Hirt once described worship in a diagram I call the worship triangle.

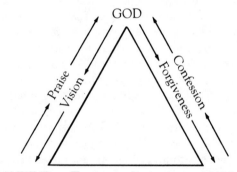

GOD

Praise
Vision

Confession
Forgiveness

MANKIND   Testimony Invitation   MAN
(corporate body) ◄——— Teaching ———► (individual)

The personal nature of the worship experience makes it difficult to describe. Many persons have deep, meaningful worship experiences in a structured worship service; others prefer such experiences when they are alone. Since all believers have been called to public worship, we need to think through the ingredients that make worship meaningful.

Because of theology, local practices, cultural influences, and historical precedents, believers down through history have expressed their worship in many different ways. These

[5]Paul Waitman Hoon, *The Integrity of Worship* (Abingdon Press, Nashville, Tenn., 1971), p. 77.

variances lie between the elaborate, prescribed rituals used in the Roman Catholic Church and the practically nonstructured Quaker meetings. Most free-worship churches lie somewhere between these two extremes, but a significant attitude and procedure problem has developed.

Marvin Hein, an eminent Mennonite Brethren pastor, described this problem as 'spectatoritis.' He said, "We sit back, fold our arms, and say to the leader of worship, 'Go ahead, excite, inspire, and hypnotize me into any mood you believe will help me. I dare you."

Because this passive, closed-door attitude is prevalent today, the believer must rethink worship and its relationship to the nurture of his Christian life.

Worship must include communion with God. For this to be real, it must be an active experience. The worship triangle shows involvement on three dimensions. One is the individual experience of man with God. Confessions of sin can be made only by an individual, not by another person or a group of persons. Thus a renewal of his self-commitment to God is individual and personal. When an individual confesses his sin, the reciprocal act is that God forgives his sin. This type of Godward motion can be expressed in the second dimension as a group of believers. Together we praise and offer our adoration to God. In return we receive a vision for service.

The third dimension involves the process of sharing the Christ experience with others. When we join together to practice the presence of God, our worship becomes not a duty but a wonder and delight. Our ascription of worth to God then becomes a tremendous power. It helps us to understand that worship is *worth-ship*. The German word for woship is "Gottesdienst," meaning "God's work" or "God's service," which aptly describes worship as an active and functional activity.

Worship may be described as a natural expression resulting from a feeling of awe or a sense of dependence upon the Creator. These expressions of worship must be nurtured, for within them lie the source of the continued, deep, spiritual life. Should worship be stifled or inhibited, a person's Christ-experience will wither, and the desire for worship will atrophy. No matter how inspiring the music or sermon, or how beautiful the sanctuary, when a church ceases to truly worship, its once spirit-filled life languishes and dies.

Why Should We Worship?

It is a commandment of the Lord.

> Give unto the Lord the glory due unto his name: bring an offering, and come before him: worship the Lord in the beauty of holiness (I Ch. 16:29).
>
> All the earth shall worship thee, and shall sing unto thee; they shall sing to thy name (Ps. 66:4).
>
> O come, let us worship and bow down: let us kneel before the Lord our maker (Ps. 95:6).
>
> But the hour cometh, and now is, when the true worshippers shall worship the Father in spirit and in truth: for the Father seeketh such to worship him. God is a Spirit: and they that worship him must worship him in spirit and in truth (Jn. 4:23–24).

In Christianity, man reestablishes in Jesus Christ the relationship that was broken by sin. The word *religion* expresses this. It is made up of the root word *lig* as in *ligament* and *re* meaning "again," such as in repeat, restore, and renew. Thus Christianity as a religion heals spiritual wounds, binds broken hearts, and builds a bridge from God to man. When this has been done, the believer has a natural desire to express praise and adoration to his Creator and Lord.

Who Can Worship?

Only a believer can worship God in the truest sense of the word. A nonbeliever cannot be expected to worship God because he does not know God as his Redeemer and Lord. He may go through the motions of singing, reading Scripture, and speaking, but until he is a born-again believer, he is not honest in his acts toward God. He is at enmity with God.

John 9:31 says, "Now we know that God heareth not sinners: but if any man be a worshipper of God, and doeth his will, him he heareth." Christian worship, then, can be expressed honestly only by a person who has confessed his sinfulness to his Creator and who has experienced the joy of knowing Him as Lord of his life.

The Christian at worship is one who acknowledges the Lordship of the risen Christ in his life. In worship, the true believer remembers that a great sacrifice was made for his salvation.

Worship is not reserved for one who is perfect. If it were, no one would qualify. A believer enters a church sanctuary with all his social pressures, ambitions, and hurts. He is a sinner, saved by grace. In worship he is energized by the Holy Spirit, who helps him along in his daily life. In worship, the believer's inner wounds may be healed and the reality of the world around him may be revealed.

How Shall We Worship?

As psychological beings, we are affected by many types of stimuli. Since worship is an experience of the whole person, the sanctuary, the music, the words we pray, the sermon we hear all affect our attitudes toward worship.

In our private devotions we can sit, stand, or kneel, just as we please. Our personal agenda simply guides the pace and content of our actions. But in corporate worship we act and feel together as one body. In order to achieve this and avoid chaos, there must be a reasonable amount of consensus regarding the group's objectives, practices, words, and actions. This leads to the question, "Do we know why we are doing what we are doing when we are together?"

As a young person from a congregation that followed simple worship patterns, I had thought of liturgical services as being cold and impersonal. I wondered about the mechanical acts of kneeling, standing, sitting, and reciting from scattered portions in the prayer book. I felt that would hinder spiritual experience. But I saw another side while serving temporarily as choirmaster for the Angelica Lutheran Church in Los Angeles.

This new experience in a liturgical worship led me to a few simple observations. I noticed that in a liturgical church the parishioner participates more actively in worship. He sings, prays, reads Scripture, and responds audibly throughout the service. The liturgists say they kneel to pray, stand to praise, and sit to listen. Bodily posture is used as an aid to remind them what is happening while they worship. About the only participation a worshiper has in most nonliturgical services is the singing of hymns and the occasional responsive readings.

The one problem with the use of liturgy is that its unchanging aspects at times become routine and lose some of their vitality. People then go through the prescribed motions without the motivations of the Holy Spirit.

The fear of the free, nonliturgical church seems to be that of falling into an esthetically beautiful but unalterably rigid worship service. There is further apprehension that an elaborate service would inhibit the moving of the Holy Spirit. Hoon clearly describes the problem.

> In the worship of certain free churches the fear of the Puritans has been vindicated: the God of Beauty has displaced the God of Christian revelation. The attributes of deity which Christian thought must insist upon—the personal character of God, his holiness, his active righteousness, his moral will, his judgment and mercy—are displaced by a vision of God as Beauty. . . .
> Predictably, the action of worship at its very core in turn becomes corrupted. Appreciation and impression become the proper response rather than decision. Contemplation is more fitting than commitment . . . [6]

Basically, the nonliturgical church has a less elaborate order of service. But it is deluded if it feels that in its simple order of worship it is nonliturgical, for a rigid adherence to any form of worship, simple or elaborate, is in fact liturgical. The so-called nonliturgical church, therefore, needs to take a new look at its worship services. It may find that

[6]Paul Waitman Hoon, *The Integrity of Worship* (Abingdon Press, Nashville, Tenn., 1971), p. 68.

most of its services are spectator oriented, passive in affecting a response, and ambiguous in purpose and design.

I often observe an appalling number of people who sleep during a worship service. If one believes that worship is a heartfelt communion with God and with one another, it should be impossible for him to sleep during worship. For many, this is like the deacon who lifts his head sleepily and says to himself, "Yes, he is still preaching the Word," then closes his eyes and contentedly falls asleep again. For such a person, a worship service is just a slot of time during the week, not a spiritual experience of the heart. Worship cannot happen without response.

Often, just being in church on Sunday morning makes us feel that we are doing our Christian duty. This habit of complacently going to church on Sunday morning seems to satisfy the feeling that as Christians we have done the right thing. But the activity of true worship involves more *giving* than it does *getting.* Our active participation—what we are willing to contribute as well as what we expect to receive—will decide what the worship service will mean to us. Most of our churches are so passive that the congregation responds more to an emotional story within a sermon than to the beauty and thrill of the total worship experience. It takes thought, work, practice, desire, alterness, and awareness to enter the deeper experience of worship. Most of us are not willing to pay such a price.

Many pastors have a superficial understanding of the possibilities inherent in the order of worship. Seminaries have failed to give proper attention to this aspect of the pastor's training. Church musicians, on the other hand, have shown much more interest in this area, because they must know why an order of worship exists in order to effectively plan the music for it. Many pastors would be hard pressed to give a rationale for the sequence of their order of worship.

Topical or Unified Service

There are various ways in which orders of worship can be organized. Many feel that usually the topical service comes closest to being ideal. This means that the Scripture reading, hymns, anthem, and sermon all are centered on one topic such as Christian living, God's grace, His loving care, His second coming, the joy of the Lord, and so on.

This type of service, also called the unified service, is effective in that it reinforces a truth in many ways. This approach makes it possible for minister and musicians to work together in finding music and Scriptures to undergird a certain topic. The problem with this approach is that the sermons have to be planned weeks in advance so the musicians have adequate time to prepare their music. Furthermore, there is always the possibility that the worship theme will not relate to the need of some persons on that particular Sunday.

Mood Service

A second approach could be called a mood service. This means that the service leads people from one experience to another based on a predetermined scriptural or psychological pattern. Cannot the Holy Spirit use our emotions and thought processes during worship? He can. He does. He must. The classic biblical example of this type of service is found in Isaiah 6:1–8. Here the parishioner is led from experiences of praise through confession and forgiveness to a point of dedication in the following way:

Praise	Holy, holy, holy is the Lord of hosts: the whole earth is full of his glory (v. 3).
Confession	Woe is me! for I am undone; because I am a man of unclean lips, and I dwell in the midst of a people of unclean lips (v. 5).
Forgiveness	Thine iniquity is taken away, and thy sin purged (v. 7).
Dedication	Whom shall I send, and who will go for us? Then said I, Here am I; send me (v. 8).

The advantage of this service pattern is that it can speak to all people regardless of background, feelings, and experiences of the week. The casual reader of this Scripture may overlook that there was a crisis in Israel. That was the year that King Uzziah died, a time of calamity for Isaiah and for Israel. Isaiah recognized that the death of the king created a critical situation, and his only hope was to turn to God in worship.

We should come to church with this same attitude. We need to come, as Isaiah did, not to hear the choir nor the pastor, nor only to see our friends, but primarily to seek the Lord. When we come together as a congregation, with all our different experiences of the week, nothing brings us together more meaningfully than when we focus our attention on God.

Obviously, this takes preparation. Worship cannot be snatched out of the air after the preacher begins talking. Worship doesn't rest in the preacher. We are together in God's house to sense the Presence of God, not the presence of a man. If we have not been prepared, we do not worship. Furthermore, we cannot prepare to worship while the pastor is preaching. Then it is too late.

A pastor once asked his congregation what they saw during worship. He related his question to Elizabeth Barrett Browning's sensitive words:

Earth's crammed with heaven,
And every common bush afire with God;
But only he who sees takes off his shoes—
The rest sit round it and pluck blackberries.

When we come to worship, do we see God or do we see blackberries? I think that many of us sit and review the labor of the week, or we daydream about a party we went to the night before when we ought to be quieting our hearts before God. We may be "plucking blackberries" more than seeing God. But when we focus on sensing the Presence of God and seeing who He is, we open the door for a refreshing experience of worship.

When we see God as Isaiah did, we see ourselves by comparison and realize how finite and faltering we are. Only then will we say, "Woe is me for I am undone." When

Isaiah saw himself, he talked about having unclean lips. But he didn't mean that he had been using profanity or foul language. He meant that he and his people had played loose with truth, honesty, and faithfulness to one another. Like James in his letter, he realized that the tongue is an unruly, evil member. It needs cleansing.

The following prayer might aid us toward a more meaningful worship. "Dear God, we know we belong to this world and You have placed us here in order to clean up the mess and build your kingdom. We're sorry to say that we have fallen down on the job."

Isaiah gives us concrete evidence that worship isn't a one-way street. Not only did Isaiah confess his sins, but God responded to that confession with these beautiful words: "Thine iniquity is taken away and thy sin purged." It isn't enough to confess our sins. We must know that He forgives. There has to be assurance of sins forgiven. How often we must come to God and say, "Father, You placed us in this world to help remedy its wrongs, and instead we have become a part of the problem." True worship will come when we pray this from the heart and know that God accepts our confession and forgives us.

One more thing happened before Isaiah was finished with his worship. When the Lord asked, "Whom shall I send, and who will go for us?" we read that Isaiah answered, "Here am I; send me." A free and relieved soul feels the exultation of having been cleansed, and this leads the believer to a point of service and commitment.

This should happen to us. We, too, come out of an insecure world. We recognize the presence of God. We confess our sins and experience cleansing. And then we say, "I'm going back to the world again, to my daily life, and by God's grace, I'll try again. I'll try to be a part of the answer rather than part of the problem."

What would happen to a congregation if this happened each Sunday? Such a congregation would become a mighty force for God in any community anywhere in the world. When a worship service encompasses purposeful design and personal involvement, the worshiper comes to church with anticipation and excitement. By contrast, many nonliturgical worship services are simply religious programs with items included for the sake of variety. In such cases there is no true "drama" of worship.

The following additional examples taken from church bulletins illustrate the framework upon which meaningful worship services have been built.

1. The Adoration of God
   The Communion with God
   The Dedication to God

2. Praise
   Confession
   Inspiration
   Dedication

3. The Preparation for Worship
   The Worship of God Through Praise
   The Worship of God Through Giving
   The Worship of God Through Communion
   The Worship of God Through Guidance
   The Worship of God Through Dedication

4. Service of Praise
   Service of Prayer
   Service of Guidance

5. We approach God reverently
   We praise God gratefully
   We beseech God humbly
   We hear God prayerfully
   We obey God willingly

6. Celebration of Hope
   Celebration of Grace
   Celebration of Fellowship
   Celebration of Thanksgiving
   Celebration of Good News

7. (Advent Service)
   Expectation
   Revelation
   Communication
   Meditation
   Benediction

8. (Liturgical—Lutheran)
   The Preparation
   We Welcome the Savior
   The Savior speaks to us
   We offer ourselves to God through Christ

Experimental Service

It would be well for us to experiment with fresh, new forms of worship. By this I do not mean that we experiment with worship itself, but rather with the ways in which worship can best be expressed. By precept, the nonliturgical church should have greater freedom than the liturgical church in finding new ways to make worship more relevant and meaningful. Strangely, it has been the liturgical church that often has been more innovative.

Some churches are exploring the area of multimedia— the use of lights, drama, pantomime, dance, art, film, and music to accentuate ideas and concepts of worship. A note of caution, however, should be sounded here, since there is a tendency among some groups to go beyond the realm of judicious taste and true spiritual worship. Our motivation should be to effect a deeper spiritual experience in worship. A worship service ceases to be worship when it becomes primarily a show.

Whatever we do, we must continually remind ourselves that the purpose of the church and worship is to relate men to Christ and to relate men in Christ to one another.

Charismatic Renewal Service

In the late 1950's and early 1960's evidence of a new style of worship began to emerge worldwide in many mainline denominations. Small groups of believers would meet in homes for a type of prayer meeting/worship experience now known as "a Charismatic fellowship." A recent poll conducted by *Christianity Today* reveals that 19 percent of all Americans (more than 29 million) consider themselves to be Pentecostal or charismatic.[7] Richard Champion, manag-

[7]Kenneth S. Kantzer, "The Charismatics Among Us." *Christianity Today*, Feb. 22, 1980, p. 25.

ing editor of the *Pentecostal Evangel,* estimates a more conservative figure of up to 10 million charismatics in this country and nearly 50 million worldwide.[8] In addition to those who consider themselves members of one of three dozen Pentecostal denominations, charismatics are found in denominations such as Methodist, Presbyterian, Baptist, Mennonite, Episcopalian, Lutheran, Roman Catholic, and many other groups. Because of the worldwide scope of this "charismatic renewal," it is imperative for the unity and communication within the church that a proper understanding of charismatic worship practices be gained and appreciated.

For many believers the charismatic renewal has brought with it a fresh understanding of what worship was really meant to be. Both the more formal, liturgical churches and those in which worship is freer, have always sought to express their worship with meaning and feeling. Unfortunately, many people have perceived their worship experiences, though outwardly proper and beautiful, inwardly void and unimaginative, lacking freshness and life-giving spirituality. Many books have been written on the subject of worship in attempts to enhance the meaning of worship by emphasizing its design, prayers, music, and so forth. Still, many churches continue unaffectedly to conduct their services unchanged, leaving a weak impact upon the life of the worshiper. The problem has not necessarily been with the words, actions, and procedures used, but that the inner nature of true worship is neither understood nor experienced as alive and vibrant.

Charistmatic renewal has brought a fresh wind of the Spirit to many worship services, giving them new vitality and meaning. The genuine tone of worship within the renewal draws its authenticity and form from the past, rekindling these forms with new spirit and significance. We might say it is "worship-worship," not "doing-worship."

Recent liturgical movements have emphasized understanding and adherence to ever-stricter liturgical design as a

[8]Richard Champion, "Those Fast-Growing Pentecostals," *Christian Leader,* June 3, 1980, p. 9.

means to enhance worship. On the other hand, the free-worship churches, in their effort to be distinctly different from the liturgical churches, consciously have emphasized a more informal worship experience. Obviously, in the more informal setting, many believers have found their needs met with a more personal approach to the worship of God. In their attempt "not to be bound," this has often lapsed into a lackluster, shallow sameness that is as empty of power as the liturgical conformity from which they were seeking escape. In their search for a more personal worship encounter, they have given their services a folksy and overly familiar character, losing the sense of God's transcendence—and with it, a depth and dignity that should always be at the heart of Judeo-Christian worship. Earnest attempts have been made to relate to neighbors—sing songs in folk language, shake hands with those around, deliver sermons in conventional style with commentaries on the events of the week in an attempt to be more "relevant." When services still became dull, pastors usually felt that greater spirituality would be achieved by making the worship atmosphere even more informal. And to make the service more spirited (albeit not more spiritual), the songs were sung ever louder and faster. Somewhere, amidst all of these good intentions, the worship and praise of God lost objective significance.

The charismatic-renewal service has restored an emphasis upon dynamic worship, in both a personal and corporate way. It has combined two important traditions found in the worship practice of the Old Testament. On the one hand, the temple tradition represents the sacrificial means to the worship of God. In the temple, the Sadducees performed their function as priests in pure, objective worship. Before the Holy of Holies, contemplative expressions of adoration and worship to God were made in the offering of the sacrifices, *for,* but separated *from,* the people. Today the Roman Catholic and Orthodox worship finds its roots in this tradition.

The other Old Testament tradition is focused on the worship of the synagogue. The Pharisees, as representatives of the prophetic school, emphasized the teaching of the

Word, i.e., worshiping with one's attention to The Book. The Protestant churches generally follow this synagogue tradition with its cognitive and subjective use of worship.

Though the Sadducees and Pharisees were not always on friendly terms, it is incorrect to think of these two schools or traditions as distinct from or hostile to each other. Nor did one merely tolerate the other. Rather, worship in the temple and worship in the synagogue each complemented the other, each fulfilling what was lacking in the other in order to give the worshiper a more complete encounter with the Living God. Indeed, the synagogues in Israel and around the Diaspora were built facing the temple of Jerusalem, and within the actual temple compound at least five synagogues were established for daily services. These were the actual "preaching places" where our Lord taught. Both traditions were understood to be important and each had a respect for the other's emphasis and purpose. It is interesting to note that charismatic renewal appears to take some of the best of these two traditions and bring them into a fresh, new "working relationship" within the framework of Christianity.

TWO OLD TESTAMENT WORSHIP TRADITIONS AND THEIR PRESENT-DAY CHRISTIAN COUNTERPARTS

Temple Tradition (*Sadducees*)   *Synagogue Tradition* (*Pharisees*)

Priest	Prophet
Objective Worship	Subjective Worship
Contemplative	Cognitive
Catholic and *Orthodox*	*Protestant*

WORSHIP WITHIN THE CHARISMATIC RENEWAL

As stated earlier, the tradition of the synagogue—office of the prophet—is best represented today in the worship experience of the Protestant Church, and the tradition of the temple—the office of the priest—is best represented by the worship of the Catholic/Orthodox churches. Since charismatic worship draws from both traditions, its worship expression has not been bound by denominational barriers. A natural ecumenicity has taken place that had not been preplanned or predicted. Furthermore, its worship service tends to be more inclusive than the traditional Protestant service. Persons of all ages, married and single, with varying theological, ethnic, and cultural backgrounds, find in charismatic worship "a place to worship God," bringing with them the distinctives of their backgrounds. And the result? Not an eclectic free-for-all, but a truly ecumenical worship arising, not from scholars writing up new experimental and ecumenical orders of worship, but from the very hearts of the worshipers themselves, seeking above all else the unity of the Spirit.

A common freedom and excitement of praise is often found wherever charismatics worship. Their service draws expressions and participation, not only from the worship leaders, but also from the worshipers. Thus, the action of worship firmly takes place from within the worshiping congregation. A type of "guided spontaneity" prevails, in which events in the service are anticipated but not prescribed or predicted. Ideally, the service is to flow freely in response to the leading of the Holy Spirit; however, this doesn't mean that the service has no director or direction. Those in charge of the meeting are responsible to guide the meeting within the guidance of the Spirit, to offer the "free-flowing river" banks for direction and content. A good charismatic service will always be a warm blending and balance of direction, content, and emotional response.

The quasi-structure of the service allows for a type of freedom and spontaneity of worship in which the pastor does not feel he needs to be in total control of the progress of the meeting. It is expected that unexpected directional changes will occur in the service, as guided by the Spirit. The people's sharing of prayer requests, testimonies, expressions of praise, as well as intermittent and spontaneous singing of hymns or choruses, bespeak a type of heart-language of the people. The exposition of the Word of God often is a shared experience. The minister prepares a sermon for the service, but time is likewise given for the

People of the Word to share with their fellow-believers. The Word of God is anticipated, not only from the lips of the preacher, but also from within the community gathered around that Word. The following brief description of such a meeting in Scotland is typical of such meetings held anywhere:

> The meeting opens with a Bible reading and talk. Then we share prayer requests, etc., before we begin to pray. During the prayer time, which on average is one and a quarter hours, there is confession, praise, intercession and singing. But people are free to manifest any of the gifts of the Holy Spirit. Frequently there are visions, prophecy, speaking in tongues and interpretation, the ministry of laying on of hands for a variety of needs, the gift of knowledge, the gift of faith, the gift of discernment and singing with the Spirit. There is an orderly freedom to pray and praise and minister as one is led by the Spirit.[9]

Rev. Robert Stamps, chaplain of Oral Roberts University and a Methodist minister, has nurtured a charismatic worship style that permits spontaneity and still retains its historic shape of Christian worship. Webber states that "what Robert Stamps has done at Oral Roberts University has been accomplished through a thorough commitment to the study of worship and a recovery of the past shaped around the experience and need of His people."[10] Ranaghan sees this campus experience as:

> first of all a desire to worship God in fullness, a desire to celebrate the mystery of Christ's death and resurrection and thereby to be nourished. Secondly, it shows an openness to discovering the deep reality of Christ's saving action as he comes to us through Word and rite.... Thirdly, one must notice how well this liturgy is integrated with the life style of

[9]G. Gordon Strachen, "Pentecostal Worship in the Church of Scotland, Part 2" (*Liturgical Review*, Scottish Academic Press, Scotland, November 1973), p. 34.

[10]Robert E. Webber, *Common Roots* (Grand Rapids, Mich.: Zondervan Publishing House, 1978), p. 103.

its worshiping community, how their faith life has both created this worship from experience and been simultaneously deepened by it. This is worship from life, oral, spontaneous, yet finding roots in the tradition of the church.[11]

Praise is more than simply one of the many ingredients of charismatic worship—it is the milieu, the whole. The scriptures declare that believers are to praise God, for it is His desire to be worshiped.[12]

But thou art holy, O thou that inhabitest the praises of Israel (Psalms 22:3).

It is a good thing to give thanks unto the Lord, and to sing praises unto thy name, O most High: to shew forth thy lovingkindness in the morning, and thy faithfulness every night, upon an instrument of ten strings, and upon the psaltery; upon the harp with a solemn sound (Psalms 92:1–3).

Praise ye the Lord: for it is good to sing praises unto our God; for it is pleasant; and praise is comely (Psalms 147:1).

Praise, ye the Lord. Praise God in his sanctuary: praise him in the firmament of his power . . . Let every thing that hath breath praise the Lord. Praise ye the Lord (Psalms 150:1, 6).

Praise enthrones Him in the hearts of His people, and is good for both the worshiper and the Worshiped One alike.

Charismatics express the spirit of joy and adoration by the raising of hands, enthusiastic but winsome singing of hymns and choruses, exclamations of verbal praise, and at times, even in spontaneous spiritual dance. Charismatic worship, perhaps more than any other within historic Christianity, is an expression of the whole person.

The study of God's Word is emphasized in contemporary charismatic worship experiences. Most charismatics find a new joy and enthusiasm in the study of the Bible; hence, in their worship, Bible reading is central. However, along with

[11]Kevan Ranaghan, "The Liturgical Renewal at Oral Roberts University", *Studia Liturgica*, Vol. 9, 1973, p. 125.

[12]For further reading on this subject see E. Judson Cornwall, *Let Us Praise* (Plainfield, N.J.: Logos International, 1973).

the centrality of the Word, many are reemphasizing the concern of the early Church and the Reformation that the Word and the Sacraments belong together. There is a fresh emphasis on the importance of the Eucharist that is appearing within the charismatic renewal. Undoubtedly, the liturgical churches have had their influence at this point. The Eucharist allows the church, not only its highest expression of praise before and in response to God's unspeakable gift, but affords the communicant an opportunity and a place for the appropriation of that which Word and Sacrament speak and promise.

The major theological distinctive within the charismatic renewal is its reemphasis upon the role of the Spirit within the life of the church and, to our interest, particularly in the worship of the People of Praise. All charismatics speak of the "baptism of the Holy Spirit" as their experience, though they would differ as to what they mean by the term. The classic Pentecostal would speak of a separate experience following conversion—an enduement of power and for the purpose of praise by the indwelling Holy Spirit, evidenced by objective gifts of the Spirit, particularly glossolalia, or speaking in tongues. Charismatics within the mainline denominations would also speak of the baptism of the Holy Spirit, but not necessarily as separate from their conversion. They would teach of a deeper work of the Spirit within their hearts and within their life as a community, releasing the gifts of the Holy Spirit for mutual edification, including the more common "prayer language," or glossolalia.

Some charismatics would be distinguished from classic Pentecostals in that the former would not see speaking in tongues as commensurate to the baptism of the Holy Spirit. Most would, in fact, identify the baptism of the Holy Spirit as their conversion, and their experience with the Holy Spirit in charismatic renewal as releasing personally and corporately that which was already resident within them by the indwelling Spirit.

Prayer and the moving of the Holy Spirit are central to worship within charismatic renewal. Most traditional churches believe and speak of the gifts of the Holy Spirit;

however, within the renewal, these expressions are taken more seriously and are held to be practical and useful for today. Emphasis is given to the conviction that the Holy Spirit should be a powerful force in every Christian's life and within the corporate life of the Body of Christ thus imparting spiritual gifts of faith, prophecy, word of knowledge, tongues, and healing.[13]

As with all pietistic revivals of the past, a new hymnody has emerged in the charismatic renewal. Usually, these songs are short, have a contemporary musical style, and can be described as Biblically oriented, or "Scripture songs." (For example: *Father, We Adore You* (Terrye Coelho), *Seek Ye First The Kingdom of God* (Karen Lafferty), and *Thou Art Worthy* (Pauline Mills). These songs have been shown to have great appeal to Christians in general—even finding their way into the worship services of some who vigorously oppose the charismatic movement itself. These songs are used across church and denominational boundaries—wherever the fires of renewal are burning. In fact, because of the broad appeal of these songs, it probably is an overstatement to say that there is a distinct "charismatic renewal hymnody." Frequently, instruments such as guitars, drums, and tambourines are used in addition to piano and organ to accompany the singing of these songs.

The charismatic movement unfortunately has within it the seeds of extremism. Excessive emotionalism by some groups has adversely depicted the movement as shallow and sentimental. When strong emotionalism has inhibited reason and intellect, distorted life-styles and worship practices have developed. At times, the evangelistic ferver of those who have received their "personal Pentecost" has caused division and hurt within congregations of believers. When spiritual arrogance has surfaced, true worship has suffered.

The charismatic movement, essentially, did not start something new. Rather, it quickened and enlivened qualities of life that were originally formed in the freshness and vitality of the Spirit of God. Worship need never become

---

[13]For additional reading on this subject see Robert G. Tuttle, Jr., *The Partakers,* (Nashville, Tenn.: Abington Press, 1974).

boring and lifeless—the Holy Spirit has come to the church so that abundant life will be the continual reality. Worship grows stale and impotent as the result of neglect and the lack of definition. Holy Spirit-led worship will always be fresh and invigorating, because the Spirit of God is constantly redefining and reexpressing the praises offered to the dynamic and living God.

Music in Worship

It may seem strange that while we are considering church music, most of this chapter should concern itself with the "nonmusical" discussion of the worship service itself. But music is not an isolated factor in worship. Rather, it is a part of a total experience. First, the service must have a purposeful design, then music attaches itself to this design to enhance its meaning.

What is the Function of Music in a Worship Service

Music has a great power for communication. Its basic function in worship is to intensify the significance of the service. Some music may serve as an aid to active worship. This is observed clearly in the musical offertory, choir anthem, solo special, and organ prelude and postlude. These intensify the worship experience of the listener. If a person is not already worshiping, however, this music becomes a harmless sound. Should our minds wander and not focus upon God, the music may be a bothersome intrusion. But to the one who meditates, prays, and considers God in all aspects, music reinforces the inspiration and enlightenment of the moment.

Music, such as congregational responses, hymn singing,[14] and service music, serves as an act of worship and becomes personally expressive. Here the parishioner en-

[14]For a practical study of the use of hymns in worship see Harry Eskew and Hugh T. McElrath, *Sing With Understanding*, (Broadman Press, Nashville, Tenn., 1980) pp. 219–242.

gages in worship by participating in "the making of music." (See Eph. 5:19 and Col. 3:16).

Music also has the possibility of assisting in the instruction of faith. Throughout church history people have learned about God's love, the great doctrines of their faith, and the claims of Christ upon their lives through music. Sometimes we falter for the words with which to express our feelings. Music helps us to put the two together.

Someone has said that music is an outward expression of an inward feeling. Since music is used in our service, with or without words, we must admit that it has great power to affect our emotions. One of the psychological functions of music in a worship service is to create a worshipful atmosphere. This presupposes the correct choice of music, adequate preparation of the music, and a meaningful performance. Since even textless music can stimulate our thinking, it is a wonderful tool to spark the imagination, make the heart receptive, and break down barriers between us and God. The problem is that most people do not understand its far-reaching power. Music as a language has the opportunity of transcending barriers that ordinarily keep men from communicating with one another. Sacred music has the unique ability to unite believers of varied biases, feelings, aspirations, and hopes, bringing them together in a common bond of love and devotion for one another and for God.

Music in the worship service is a tool that induces serious participation. The reason many people do not become involved in our worship services is that there is little opportunity for personal participation. The passive attitude and sleeping mind attest to this noninvolvement. When I see people sleeping in a worship service, I wonder if the Lord would ask them, as He did His disciples, "What, could ye not watch with me one hour?" (Matt. 26:40). If God's judgment upon the Israelites is any indication of the seriousness of worship, we dare not take lightly our acts of worship lest they too become a mockery.

The Lord condemned Israel, saying, "I hate, I despise your feasts, and I take no delight in your solemn assemblies. Even though you offer me your burnt offerings and cereal offerings, I will not accept them, and the peace offerings of your fatted beasts I will not look upon. Take away from me the noise of your songs; to the melody of your harps I will not listen. But let justice roll down like waters, and righteousness like an everflowing stream." (Amos 5:21–24).

No matter what form our outward worship takes, all is in vain unless our worship is a sincere expression of the heart. For after all, God looks upon the heart. (See 1 Sam. 16:7.)

If we believe that music is important in the service, then it is imperative that we consider the type of music used. The most important is the music text. The psalmist said: "Thou hast magnified thy word above all thy name" (Ps. 138:2). Music in this case is the servant of the text—a bearer of the words. Which is the more important—the serving tray, or the delicious fruit it carries?

When choosing music for worship, we should ask the following questions: Are the texts of the hymns and anthems scripturally and theologically correct? Are the text and music compatible with the design of the worship service? Is the text inspiring literature? Does the music enhance the meaning of the words or does it call attention to itself?

Music is like a glass window. It keeps out the threatening weather of discordant life, while it allows us to look out to see the opportunities of service which lie beyond the confines of our enclosed area of living. Thus it opens new vistas of understanding and experience. Music is also like a glass prism through which God's eternal verities shine. It breaks this light into a spectrum of many beautiful truths. Music may be a skylight that allows the light of Christ to come into our lives, giving light to the daily walk. Music may also be a mirror to help us to see who we really are and to give us an opportunity to assess our own spiritual lives.

Where do we stand in our understanding of Christian worship? How can music best be used in it? Is worship a program in which there are simply a series of items of interest? Or is it drama that says something real, living, and eternal? People commonly view the choir and preacher as actors in the drama of worship. God, the Holy Spirit, is the Prompter; and the spectators are the congregation. This type of worship is not God centered. It leads to self-glorification and spiritual stagnation. Kierkegaard[15] suggests that true drama of worship occurs when the worshipers in the congregation are the actors, the preacher and the choir are the prompters, and God is the Listener. Only then is it life-giving, God-honoring worship.

[15]Sören Kierkegaard, *Purity of Heart*. Tr. Douglas V. Steere (New York: Harper and Brothers, Torchbooks, 1956), 177–184.

New Sounds in Church Music

History reveals that the church was born and lives in the midst of struggle and tension. These tensions have continually manifested themselves in music.

The admonitions of both the Old and New Testaments regarding the use of music by believers seem to indicate that the tensions even in biblical days led to apparent misuses of music. The church does not live in a vacuum nor did it then. The believer is subject to the influences of the sociocultural changes of society just as is the nonbeliever.

The church, however, in assessing its needs, continually has tried to sift the forces of society to find those that contribute to its life-blood. The tools and methods it has adopted as a part of its life-style have at times become distorted and abused, but the church has continually sought to reevaluate these tools in order to be more effective in her world mission. Consequently, there have always been new sounds in church music, simply because music in society has continually changed. Admittedly, changes in church practice have not come easily. The acceptance of new methods, procedures, and sounds are usually slow. The church generally has been reluctant to use new methodology and tools, fearing that it may be tampering with the unchanging gospel.

The Christian church's struggle with the changing patterns of music performance and composition began in its early history. By the time the Council of Laodicea convened in the fourth century, congregational singing in the worship service had become so chaotic and disruptive that it was decreed such singing would be abandoned as a part of the worship service.

For several centuries Gregorian chant, sung in unison by the clergy, was used in the worship service. One can imagine the perplexed mind of the parishioner when, as the result of the development of polyphonic music, two- and three-part music was introduced into the church during the latter part of the Middle Ages. Nevertheless, it was the church that continued to foster the arts during this period, and church musicians were in the forefront of introducing new sounds into the church.

Abuses of music also began to appear. The motet, one of the major sacred vocal forms of the latter Middle Ages, became adulterated by the inclusion of secular texts and tunes. The polyphonic techniques of writing became so complicated that in many cases the art of music overshadowed the expression of the text. As a result, the Council of Trent, during the sixteenth century, felt it necessary to reevaluate the music practices of the church. They rejected certain classes and styles of music as unsuitable for use in the Roman Catholic church.

At the same time, the Lutheran wing of the Reformation movement introduced a new sound into the church by reestablishing congregational singing with the use of the chorale. Still another voice of the Reformation movement, that of John Calvin, introduced the new sounds of the psalm tune. In the latter part of the seventeenth century, because of the deterioration of congregational singing in England, Isaac Watts envisioned a new song for the church and introduced the great English hymn.

It should be noted that the introduction of the hymn into a traditionally psalm-singing church caused a great struggle for many believers. They were not sure that man-made lyrics could adequately express the feelings, aspirations, and praises of a believer, as could the psalms of David. Once the Watts hymns became known, the Wesleyan hymn was introduced during the eighteenth century as the ministry of John and Charles Wesley swept the British Isles. The changing needs of their society called for a song that would relate to the masses and adequately speak within its own time. Indeed the hymns of the seventeenth and eighteenth centuries are still popular and regularly used.

In keeping with historical precedence, the Moody revivals of the nineteenth century also introduced a new sound into the church—the gospel song. The subsequent debate among church musicians concerning its worth has been heated and prolonged.

In the third quarter of the twentieth century, many innovations appeared on the church music scene, such as rock, folk, jazz, and electronic music, all mixed with experimental avant-garde worship expressions. We can see from this résumé that there have been many new sounds in church music throughout history. Perhaps we need not fear some new ones in our times.

It is interesting to note that evangelical churches have been trying for years to upgrade their music. While a significant part of their singing diet was the gospel song and the gospel chorus, attempts have been made during the last three decades to introduce more hymns, psalm tunes, and chorales into their congregational singing repertoire. As choir directors have become better trained, they have added anthems to the more customary hymn arrangements. The evangelical church musician may now need to revise his approach and reevaluate his position in regard to the new dimensions opening up in church music.

It is also interesting to note that during this same period of time the so-called formal churches with their more sophisticated music have done an almost complete about-face by introducing rock, jazz, and other "secular" musical elements into their services. Speaking about this phenomenon in a lecture to the National Church Music Fellowship Convention in Washington, D.C., Donald Hustad stated, "Only recently, with some self-consciousness about our history of 'evangelistic' music, we are moving toward more meaningful hymns and anthems. We had just started going uphill, when we met the competition coming down, playing guitars and singing folksongs!"

We are now at a time in the life of the church when the mood of experimentation and change is so dramatic, so intense, that a constant reevaluation must take place. It is easy to say we must face reality, look at things as they are, and be opened-minded. It is more difficult actually to become informed and to attempt to respond to the truths as they are made available. Tensions arise because on one hand we respond favorably in church to anthems, hymns, gospel songs, and organ preludes and on the other hand in our daily living world we continually hear the sounds of rock, jazz, and other types of popular music on television, radio, recordings, and in live performances. The resulting psychological effect from this listening to the air waves is so forceful we can't help become, at least in part, what we hear and see.

The stark reality of this problem comes close to home because many church musicians, as well as music educators, are unable to ascertain the psychological, physiological, sociological, and spiritual effects of prominent forms of popular music. Equally perplexing is the development of various styles and sounds resulting from avant-garde experimentation. These are compositional concepts such as bitonality (two scales played simultaneously), polytonality (several scales played simultaneously), atonality (avoidance of the playing of any standard tonal center), serial music (the playing of a prescribed series of a twelve-tone row made up of the twelve notes in an octave) and aleatoric music (pitches determined by the performer). Additional experimentation with electronic and computer music presents a milieu of sounds and styles that ultimately find their way into the church service.

The future road the church must take does not lie in the ultraconservative point of view, nor in the ultraradical position. A reconciliation of the traditional with the new must be effected. If we intend to have the church relate to a changing society, we must face the problem squarely. To do otherwise would be spiritual suicide.[1]

We know that in past years men such as Martin Luther, John Calvin, Isaac Watts, John and Charles Wesley, Ira Sankey, and many others made important contributions based upon the knowledge of their current situation. It would be a good exercise for us to make a similar analysis of our current situation, with the hope of moving ahead in our work for Christ. Possibly the most emotionally charged and

[1]For added reading on this subject see Chapter 8, "The 'Great Debate' of the 1960s and 1970s," Donald Paul Ellsworth, *Christian Music in Contemporary Witness*, (Baker Book House, Grand Rapids, Mich., 1979), pp. 146–172.

least understood problem of our day lies in the question whether church music in its varied ministries can embrace the rock idiom in its repertoire of styles. Since popular music is making a strong impact upon both secular and spiritual culture, let us briefly consider rock music.

In the late 1950's and the 1960's, such groups as the Beatles, the Doors, the Monkeys, Jefferson Airplane, the Rolling Stones, the Fifth Dimension, and personalities such as Elvis Presley became household names to a majority of our Christian young people. Within a short time the penetration of this style went beyond the home into the church as religious rock groups were formed. This sudden invasion of the rock idiom into the Christian community many times caused severe prejudicial views about this music. An understandable "church music gap" soon appeared. By contrast, during the first half of the twentieth century, especially the evangelical church generally shied away from listening and performing popular music basically because of its association with ballroom dancing and the night club—types of "worldly amusements." Unfortunately, the Christian family has not understood this new music and consequently has not been able to speak effectively on the issue.

What is the message of rock music? Why does the rock text and music hold such an intense sway over the minds of our youth? Don Wyrtzen, eminent composer and editor for Singspiration Music Co., has made some interesting observations about hard rock music. He stated that rock music is an expression of a current philosophy that claims absolute and total personal freedom including love and sex.[2] Examples of texts from rock music that express this philosophy are, "I'm going to do what I want to do. I don't care if I break some rules," and "Go where you want to go, do what you want to do, say whatever you want to say." Some of our current philosophy of education seems to contribute to this concept. From kindergarten on, a student is taught to be himself, to be uninhibited, to be free.

In contrast to this self-emphasis, Scripture teaches that we are to be reconciled with one another and God, that

---

[2]Don Wyrtzen, "Rock 'N Roll," *Lifelines* 7 (Fall 1969): 1.

there must be the sharing of our lives with one another, that we are to be burden-bearers. Being a follower of Christ means yielding to the discipline and dependency of His teaching. It leads to the recognition that our bodies are the temple of the Holy Spirit and that we are not our own. It is only in this dimension of understanding that there is a true personal freedom and a life that is released from guilt. Only then is one unshackled from the restraint of sin.

Mr. Wyrtzen also stated that rock music espouses the philosophy of existentialism or the "now" ethnic that puts a major emphasis upon the individual and his response to the present. What is important is "me—now."[3] The validity of an experience is dependent to a large degree upon how it feels *now*. Thus if there is an expanded experience, a feeling of ecstasy, a good feeling, it is all right. It follows then that music which is rational, based on previous experience and history, is not necessarily valid. The important thing is to respond to any kind of stimuli that will add to the "now" experience.

As a Christian, I view existentialism as a private standard that falls far short of God's standard. Anyone who is a Christian believer, it seems to me, willingly accepts a standard that comes from outside of himself—God's standard.

The third idea in rock music that Mr. Wyrtzen suggests is that of Eastern mysticism. This Far Eastern philosophy emphasizes "contemplation and love apart from the medium of human reason." The guru from Rishikesh, Maharishi Mahesh Yogi, has had as his students such well-known rock and folk performers as the Beatles, the Beach Boys, and Donovan. Further reflections of a Far Eastern mystical approach are noted in the *Far East Suite* and *Psychedelic Suite* by Duke Ellington, and by the performances of the Indian Ravi Shankar.

A final observation by Wyrtzen mentions that rock music is intimately connected with the drug-abuse problem. In a chaotic world where many young people do not have a purpose and seemingly cannot find an ultimate meaning, objective reality has become dull. Consequently, they turn

[3]Ibid.

to marijuana and other drugs.[4] The hippie movement of the 1960's brought many rock songs with hidden phrases and double meanings. The close involvement of sex and drug abuse with rock music makes one wonder if either could be so prevalent without the other.

The drub-abuse problem has been fed by the existentialist who sets up his own standard. Nevertheless, certain universal principles operate whether he recognizes it or not. We all need to know that we break certain laws at our own peril no matter who we are. We don't even need to read the Bible to know that the misuse of drugs breaks universal laws. Rock guitarist Jimi Hendrix died after taking an overdose of sleeping pills. Sixteen days later Janis Joplin, a rock singer, committed suicide. Joel Dreyfuss, an Associated Press newsman, describes her style of singing as "a piercing wail, a cry that seemed to come from a lonely despairing soul."[5] Janis Joplin graphically described the tremendous power of rock music following her first appearance at the Avalon, a San Francisco ballroom. "I couldn't believe it, all that rhythm and power. I got stoned just feeling it, like it was the best dope in the world. It was so sensual, so vibrant, loud, crazy. I couldn't stay still; I had never danced when I sang, but there I was moving and jumping. I couldn't hear myself, so I sang louder and louder. By the end I was wild."[6]

A young person may say that rock music does not affect him. However, studies dealing with the psychology of music indicate that many kinds of bodily responses react to the stimulus of music. There is no way to escape or insulate the bodily response from the pulsating power of rock music.

The *Washington Post,* July 19, 1968, comments on the words of Marye Mannes, a cultural critic who calls acid rock "the new illiteracy, and the young love it. They love it because they would rather feel than think. It is easier. It is also easier for those who cater to them. For, to blast the senses—to blow the mind—you don't need training. You

[4]Wyrtzen, p. 2.

[5]Joel Dreyfuss, "Janis Joplin Followed the Script," *Wichita Eagle,* October 6, 1970, p. 7A.

[6]Quoted by Dreyfuss, p. 7A.

don't need knowledge. You don't even need talent. All you need is a boundless ego, a manic temperament, and the loudest amplifying equipment you can get. Then you can do your own thing." She further commented, "There is some very real talent in the contemporary arts. But there is a world of difference between, say, Simon [and] Garfunkel or Peter, Paul and Mary, and this riot of the soul. And like all riots, it is essentially destructive and degrading." Her conclusion: "If the essence of creative expression is to bring meaning and beauty into life, then the sound and fury of the new illiteracy is bent on destroying both."[7]

In the late 1970's, disco music emerged from rock music, receiving a tremendous musical thrust in the movie *Saturday Night Fever,* and in the music of the Bee Gees, Diana Ross, Donna Summers, and many others. This time, instead of appealing only to the young people, disco addressed itself also to the white-collar working class such as teachers, salespeople, clerical workers, etc. The intense adherence to disco by its followers resembles a type of religion. Its nonstop dance music provides a hedonistic atmosphere with its pulsating heat, emphasizing the soaring high-frequency sounds of synthesizers, brass, and soprano voices, augmented with various special effects such as rotating mirror balls, pulsing lights, strobes, lasers, holograms, fog, and neon. This inordinantly sensual stimulation provides an attractive fantasy escape and discotheques have become a haven for homosexuals and persons with various types of deviant behavior. Richard Peterson in his article "Disco!" concludes that in disco, along with jazz and rock, the medium is much of the message. His characterization of the new disco person reveals his attitude to be self-centered, self-reliant, and ostentatious.

I am good. I like my body, and I like what I am. I am a survivor (as pointed out by the Bee Gees in their song "Stayin' Alive"), able to thrive in an anomic urban world of strangers. I can overcome alienating work and the stigmas of

[7]Quoted by Lawrence Laurent, "ABC News Format Proves Successful," *The Washington Post,* July 19, 1968, p. C7.

race, sex, and ethnicity. The day may belong to Them, but the night is Mine. Here I am, in control, and my fantasy is real.[8]

Philip Bickel in his article "The Loss of Soul in Rock Music,"[9] chronicles the stages of the progression of rock music from its brash, optimistic beginning in 1955 with Bill Haley and the Comets' release of "Rock Around the Clock"; Elvis Presley's trek to stardom; the social-conscience expressions in the folk-music revival led by Peter, Paul, and Mary; the concurrent emergence of soul; the wrestling of young people with problems of social justice and rebellion against materialism, to the appearance of disco. A curious mixture of drugs, brotherly love, relaxed sexual mores, and religion are answers they espoused in many of their rock songs. The subsequent drug-related deaths of rock stars, the emerging violence at rock concerts, and the failure of social problems to disappear revealed the weakness and insufficiency of their approach. He states in another paper that despite their sincerity "they did not succeed because they had rejected God and His Word and had put their faith in an inadequate object—themselves. Built on an autonomous, man-centered foundation, the rock culture could not help but crumble under pressure."

The electronic age fits well into this philosophy. Electronic music, accompanied by psychedelic lights, excited rhythms, and uninhibited lyrics, presents an enormous appeal to the teenager. The hectic tempo of today's life draws the young person to where the action is. The fast-moving, rhythmic, loud, electronically amplified sounds psychologically build a feeling of excitement and thus give the sensation of actually being on the scene. It is easy to understand why young people, through extensive exposure to this form of stimuli, can be caught up with a culture that espouses this type of secularism and existential philosophy.

[8]Richard A. Peterson, "Disco!", *The Chronicle Review* supplement to *The Chronicle of Higher Education*. October 2, 1978, p. R-27.
[9]Philip Bickel, "The Loss of Soul in Rock Music," *Christianity Today,* February 22, 1980, pp. 32–33.

What have these excesses in music done to our sensitivity? Have our senses become so dulled by overexposure to mass media and loud sounds that we cannot be energized to action except by volume approaching the threshold of pain? Has the exposure to so many styles produced in us a type of aesthetic schizophrenia? Our affluent society offers so many stimuli that our lives often become too calloused to hear "the still small voice." Oswald Spengler, in his *Decline of the West,* gives us an ominous warning that "in the last stages of civilization all art becomes nothing but titillation of the senses (nerve excitement)."[10] From this perspective we should examine what we are doing and why.

What does one say in the light of these indictments? We have presented the problematic side of the picture, but it would be blindness on the part of the Christian to dismiss these arguments without giving them serious consideration. The Christian must be concerned with that which will nurture the spiritual life of the inner man. Rock music provides for many people a substitute for the so-called "turned-on" experience that Jesus Christ gives through the Holy Spirit.

The psalmist gives the real answer to this longing of the heart when he says, "Delight thyself also in the Lord; and he shall give thee the desires of thine heart" (Ps. 37:4). The permanent enrichment of the soul and excitement of life come from the placing of proper priorities. If the immediate sensual, psychological, and physical experiences are desired, then it is true that rock music can be that fulfillment for the moment. It is more true, however, that as Christians our guidelines are set in another direction that really give a lasting, satisfying experience. Paul states, "If ye then be risen with Christ, seek those things which are above, where Christ sitteth on the right hand of God. Set your affection on things above, not on things on the earth" (Col. 3:1, 2). No doubt the greatest of all experiences comes when we become partakers of the divine nature. Peter says: "His divine power hath given unto us all things that pertain unto

---

[10]As quoted by Jack Wheaton, "Are Jazz Festivals Killing Jazz?" *Pro/Ed Review* 1 (April/May 1972):19.

life and godliness, through the knowledge of him that called us to glory and virtue: whereby are given unto us exceeding great and precious promises: that by these ye might be partakers of the divine nature, having escaped the corruption that is in the world through lust" (II Peter 1:3, 4).

The best screen through which we can sift rock and all other music is given by Paul in this statement: Finally, brethren, whatsoever things are true, whatsoever things are honest, whatsoever things are just, whatsoever things are pure, whatsoever things are lovely, whatsoever things are of good report; if there be any virtue, and if there be any praise, think on these things" (Phil. 4:8). We have the biblical injunction to live circumspectly, to judge that which is evil and that which is good, and to strive for the "high calling of Jesus Christ." As critical, searching Christians we are derelict if we do not think on these things. We simply must "Prove all things; hold fast to that which is good. Abstain from all appearance of evil" (I Thes. 5:21, 22).

Historical precedence still tells us that all the music of the society in which man has lived, has in some way influenced the music he has used in his Christian experience. The street song that was transformed into the chorale during the Reformation became a new song for the church that still is being used today. The Wesleys found serviceable music for immediate communication of the gospel in the secular style of their day. Many of these hymns still are found in our major denominational hymnals. Probably the most common congregational song known by evangelicals, the gospel song, borrowed its style from the common songs of the day. Using the gospel song, Sankey's powerful voice, persuasive personality, and dramatic style became potent assisting tools in the revivals of Dwight L. Moody. Within the last decade the folk hymn has emerged as an appealing and effective tool for communicating the gospel to young people both inside and outside the church. Lloyd Pfautsch observes:

The history of church music has recurring instances when the church borrowed from its environment. The church met the people where they were and appropriated what was familiar and meaningful to the people. However, it also distilled what it borrowed in such a way that the secular associations became secondary to the primacy of worship.[11]

Rock music, even though it has had a questionable origin and practice, during the 1970's became a part of the mainstream of church music. It gradually was reshaped, refined, and adapted. Seemingly as the rhythmic excesses became more palatable and the style became more familiar, the earlier secular associations were less remembered and a gradual acceptance followed. This type of music that covers many styles has become known as "Contemporary Gospel."

Evidence of the escalation of contemporary gospel music is seen in the increasing number of professional contemporary gospel groups that concertize throughout the year on a full-time basis. Persons such as Andrae Crouch and Larry Norman have charted new musical paths of Christian musical communication. Youth organizations in thousands of churches are developing their own contemporary gospel-music groups. New life is being injected into many youth programs with the production of Christian children and youth musicals that have come off the press in voluminous numbers. Large stadiums and civic auditoriums are being filled at Christian rock concerts emulating their secular counterparts. Christian coffee houses are found in most large cities. A phenomenal growth has taken place in the number of Christian radio stations that extensively propagate contemporary gospel music. Most of the music represented in the movement is directed towards Christian outreach and is experience oriented, resulting in tremendous evangelistic efforts. Without question, musically and spiritually dead churches have experienced much benefit through these influences. On the other hand, great church music programs may have slipped in quality and become less effective.

In the light of observing both the unchristian aspects of

---

[11]Lloyd Pfautsch, "Worship and Crisis in Church Music," *Music Ministry* (November 1969), p. 5.

rock and disco music and also the positive results of using contemporary gospel music, some basic questions still lurk that need clearer answers. (1) If the medium is the message, could it be that rock music is inherently incapable of providing mature Christian messages? (2) Will our less cerebral and more experience-oriented church music have a long-term debilitating effect upon the spiritual and musical life of the believing community? (3) Is the church abdicating its role to teach the music of witness and worship to meet the total ministry of the church for all of its people? (4) Does the tremendous stress on rock and disco music cause our young people to become a "locked-in" generation, that does not allow them to open their hearts and minds to learning, understanding, and appreciating other than their own rock music? In 1971, William J. Petersen expressed the following hope:

> Young people today, most analysts agree, have a broader appreciation of music than any previous generation. If this be so, the next generation should see a wider variety of psalms, hymns and spiritual songs sung congregationally and performed by artists in church than ever before.[12]

Now, almost 10 years following the writing of the above statement and after 30 years of working directly with college young people, my impression is that this broadening of musical appreciation or understanding is not taking place. I'm not sure why. Students are not generally as open to listen and perform a broad spectrum of Christian music. Few regularly attend larger musical performances such as oratorios and cantatas. Rarely does a student become deeply interested in hymnody and in his own church hymnal. Is it that their strong commitment to contemporary gospel music does not allow them to experience music other than that which they currently know? It suggests the influence of the secular culture that says it's only what is done today that is worthy and counts.

[12]William J. Peterson, "O, What a Fantastic New Day for Christian Music," *Eternity*, April 1971, p. 52.

The many new sounds in church music become perplexing for many Christians, young and old. As we look ahead we will need the wisdom of Solomon to release ourselves from our older, ineffective practices. We will need to discern that which is still effective of the old and accept new and relevant trends. Donald Ellsworth challenges us that we "must select with care music for worship, edification, and evangelism, balancing the new with the old, the artless with the artistic, and the simple with the profound."[13] As we feel the urgency to express ourselves in contemporary forms, let us take a balanced view and be motivated by the spirit of renewal that may bring with it a rebirth of music as well.

With the ongoing task of sifting the good from the bad, reconciling the old with the new, we must keep our eyes fixed on Jesus Christ. Our understanding needs to be sensitized by the leading of the Holy Spirit, and our attitude open to ways of expressing the gospel with new sounds, colors, moods, and words. The apostle Peter clearly indicates how to develop this type of responsible attitude. "But to obtain these gifts, you need more than faith; you must also work hard to be good, and even that is not enough. For then you must learn to know God better and discover what He wants you to do. Next, learn to put aside your own desires so that you will become patient and godly, gladly letting God have his way with you. This will make possible the next step, which is for you to enjoy other people and to like them, and finally you will grow to love them deeply" (II Pet. 1:5–7, Living Bible).

[13]Donald Paul Ellsworth, *Christian Music in Contemporary Witness*, (Baker Book House, Grand Rapids, Mich. 1979), p. 199.

VI

Reevaluating Music in the Organized Church

To some people, planning for the organized church today means giving concern only to an outmoded and deteriorating organization. Admittedly, it is impossible to predict what the new face of the church will be in the future, how it will be organized, and what part music will play in its life. Nevertheless, unless a hostile political environment expressly forbids the "assembling of the saints," some type of organized church will always exist, thus there will always be a functioning program of music in the life of the church.

Values of Church Music

The following values of church music are apparent to an increasing number of church members as vital to the total ministry of the church. In the first place, church music provides an avenue of worship for the believer. People can sing their petitions, praise, adoration, intercession, and dedication to the Lord. It is the "together" experience of singing hymns and gospel songs that brings added vitality to the worship experience. Moreover, the use of choirs and instruments aids the parishioner in his acts of worship.

Church music also contributes to the spirit of witnessing and evangelism. An evangelistic church, as a rule, is a singing church. Many persons have been touched by the spirit of God and influenced toward a deeper commitment through the singing of Christian songs. A rebirth of singing has usually accompanied the great revival movements in church history.

Church music affords an opportunity for the cultivation of musical talents of church members. Since music is the means by which many Christian people use their God-given talents, the church through its adult service choir, graded choirs, and instruments makes it possible for its members to develop their musical abilities. This in turn creates a feeling of goodwill and gratitude on the part of the parishioner toward the church for providing such opportunities.

Music opens many avenues for learning since the ministry of music touches all phases of church life. Teaching Bible truths and theology, sharing testimonies, praying—all are opportunities for church music to serve as a valuable aid in learning.

Church music offers an opportunity for Christian service. Many persons have their first introductions into Christian service through the choir programs of the church. As the language of the soul, choir music helps interpret the Word of God just as the preacher does. In this sense, church music has been called the "younger brother" of the preaching of the Word. Christians with songs in their hearts find their service to God enjoyable, inspirational, and consequently more effective.

It is not my purpose here to fully discuss all aspects of church-music administration, since many excellent books treat this subject thoroughly.[1] In our rethinking of church music I would like to give attention to three phases of the continuing mission of church music: congregational singing, music in Christian education, and the role of the minister of music.

Congregational Singing

Church music accomplishes its greatest ministry through congregational singing. Because of the potential ministry of congregational singing in the life of the church, most churches strive to develop a more hymn-loving and hymn-singing congregation.[2]

[1]For a concise overview of church music administration see Vic Delamont, *The Ministry of Music in the Church* (Chicago: Moody Press, 1980).

[2]For a more detailed discussion of congregational singing see William J. Reynolds, *Congregational Singing* (Nashville, Tennessee, Convention Press, 1975).

What are the ingredients that make for spiritually satisfying congregational singing? A congregation needs to sing with both understanding and spirit. First Corinthians 14:15 says, "I will sing with the spirit, and I will sing with the understanding also." So that music can clothe the text with beauty, the congregation should try to sing musically. This does not mean reaching choir performance level, but singing becomes more enjoyable with a reasonable amount of uniformity of attacks and releases, a rhythm that is vital, has appropriate movement of tempo, and a tone quality that is firm and blending. A deeper and richer spiritual experience in congregational singing comes when all participate together, for singing is both a privilege and a responsibility. The psalmist said, "Let the people praise thee, O God; let all the people praise thee" (Ps. 67:3). All good hymnals contain a wide variety of gospel songs and hymns.[3] By singing these songs and hymns thoughtfully, a congregation has the opportunity to express itself in many moods, about many subjects, in many styles, and for a variety of purposes.

Since the Reformation period, congregational singing has given added vitality and life in worship to the gathered Christians. John Wilson speaks of its ministry today as ingoing, outgoing, and up-reaching.[4]

Congregational singing is an inward expression of "speaking to yourselves in psalms and hymns and spiritual songs" (Eph. 5:19). Even though we sing with others, its most significant meaning is to the individual person. The value of congregational singing is that even a person who is not capable of singing with great musical skill can gain inspiration, comfort, and joy.

Congregational singing also has an outward direction. The many hymns and gospel songs of testimony give opportunity for the Christian to share his faith with others. In Colossians 3:16 we are encouraged to go about "teaching

[3]The following nondenominational hymnals are a few of several published during the 1970's useful especially for free worship Protestant churches: *Hymns For The Living Church* (Hope, 1974); *Hymns For The Family of God* (Paragon, 1976); *The New Church Hymnal*, Lexicon, 1976); *Praise!* (Singspiration, 1979).

[4]John F. Wilson, *An Introduction to Church Music* (Chicago: Moody, 1965), pp. 120–121.

and admonishing one another in psalms and hymns and spiritual songs." In singing together, believers can encourage, admonish, and inspire one another. One of Martin Luther's critics recognized this power when he said, "The whole people are singing themselves into Lutheran doctrine."[5]

Another important dimension of congregational singing is the upward experience. The apostle Paul encourages us to be "singing with grace in your hearts to the Lord" (Col. 3:16). The psalmist often expressed his praise to God. We too can find much joy as Christians in our expression of praise and adoration to God. If the motivation of the heart is right, then the Lord will hear our innermost expressions, whether we have a beautifully trained voice or a stammering tongue.

The major question for most churches is, "How is better congregational singing developed?" It is clear that it cannot best be accomplished by talking, reading, or writing. Rather, we learn to sing by singing. Consequently, singing should become a common practice at all functions of the church. It is important that there be an infiltration of singing into the total life of the church. A major effect should be directed toward the training of children because they are more receptive and show quick results. Usually the appreciation level of older people is more limited than that of younger people. The singing habits of people do not alter much after the age of 40. This, however, does not mean that many older people do not learn or add to what they already know.

Several principles need to be remembered in teaching new hymns to the congregation. Expect progress to be slow, for people's habits and practices do not change overnight. It is imperative that we approach people at their level of musical understanding and work from there. In the process of starting where the people are, it is important that new hymns not be pushed too fast. A song leader cannot afford to develop a communication gap by ridiculing the hymns the congregation likes, no matter how bad he considers

[5]Quoted by John F. Wilson, *An Introduction to Church Music* (Chicago: Moody, 1965), p. 121.

them to be. A song leader who tries to impress his people with his knowledge of hymnology by talking too much will only lose his congregation. The important thing is to give emphasis continually to the devotional aspect of singing.

More specifically, the important principle of teaching new hymns is to make new tunes as familiar as possible in the shortest time and in the least painful way. To accomplish this, a common practice is to use a "hymn-of-the-month" program. One of the plans in this program is to introduce the hymn on the first Sunday of the month by having the organist play it as a prelude. The second Sunday it may be sung by the choir or a soloist. On the third and fourth Sundays it is sung by the congregation. The hymn should be sung occasionally during the following year. Hymn stories, brief articles in the church bulletin, pictures and posters on bulletin boards, all stimulate further interest in the "hymn-of-the-month" program. Some churches have successfully used congregational rehearsals of hymns before the evening service as a meaningful guide to learning. Regardless of the procedure, it is important that a song leader have a planned program with adequate materials, leaving nothing to chance or guesswork.

Naturally, problems are to be expected in trying to improve congregational singing. There may be indifference on the part of the congregation, the organist, the pianist, and at times even the clergy. Prejudices and jealousies often arise because people resist change, feeling that their importance may be threatened. If a congregation has never developed good congregational singing, a major obstacle is the ingrown timidity of the congregation. Often they are simply afraid to hear their own voices. Although developing good congregational singing is a long-term project and has many obstacles, its worth and importance to the spiritual life of a congregation make it not only worthwhile and ultimately rewarding, but also imperative.

Music in Christian Education

The music program of the church represents only one of the agencies that contribute to the total mission of the church. Music does not stand alone, nor is it set aside in its spiritual ministry. Indeed, it is a part of the total work of Sunday school, youth work, worship services, and other church activities.[6] In one sense there is not a separate music department in the church; it is a program that assists all departments of the church. Ministry gifts given to the church are not vested in one person. Rather, these gifts are varied and given to many people. Some are described as "apostles; and some, prophets; and some, evangelists; and some, pastors and teachers (Eph. 4:11)." I have thought it would be well to have included the minister of music with this list of callings. We need to realize, however, that music assists each of the callings—apostles, prophets, evangelists, pastors, and teachers. In this sense, music serves an important function in Christian education. The general purpose of Christian education is to give training and experience in evangelism, spiritual growth, and worship. These objectives also underlie the music activities of the church. Consider specifically the meetings in Christian education that take place in Sunday schools, Bible classes, and youth meetings. We need to know how music can be used effectively to support these objectives. For example, if a theme is developed for a program, it is important that music, sung or played, relate to the overall design and purpose of the program. Special stress should be given to the words and ideas expressed in music.

Music often flounders in meetings because the planning of the music is not given careful attention. Incompetent music leaders also contribute to the problem. The song leader should be a Christian with a pleasant voice who knows how to lead, persuade, and inspire people toward spiritual goals through music. Secondly, the accompanist—organist, pianist, or guitarist—should be someone who enjoys accompanying and is not primarily interested in the display of technique.

We can usually agree on the purposes of church music, but deciding on the repertoire poses some problems. In

---

[6]For a review of biblical principles in music for Christian Education see Alfred E. Lunde, *Christian Education Thru Music* (Wheaton, Illinois: Evangelical Teacher Training Assn., 1978), pp. 7–20.

considering the text of the songs used to undergird the objectives of Christian education, it is important to incorporate those that project correct spiritual concepts of God, Jesus Christ, the Holy Spirit, the Christian life, and eternal life. This in turn encourages good Christian attitudes and behavior. In Christian Education work words and ideas generally should be within a child's understanding and interest. Additionally, they should also be good from a literary standpoint. A great variety of songs need to be included—objective (Godward) along with subjective (manward), old and new, difficult and easy, spirited and contemplative, familiar and unfamiliar.

The consideration of music often is more of a problem than is the text. It usually is wise to avoid music with complex rhythms, intervals, and harmony that make group singing difficult. A singable melody line must be within comfortable vocal range. Discretion should be used concerning music style. If it contains elements of popular music to the extent that it detracts from the meaning of the words, it is not good. On the other hand, if this popular style induces participation, enhances the meaning of the words, and generally inspires people to sing when otherwise they would not, then it serves a good purpose.

At times it is good for a teacher to include music that will cause the singers to stretch their thinking and learning. Exposure to great and worthy music is always important. A good principle to remember in Christian education is that the materials and songs that young people learn, especially grade-school children, often set a standard for them the rest of their lives. It is true that much of the music used especially by children is designed specifically for their age group. Nevertheless, it is important that young persons be introduced to music that becomes more meaningful with familiarity. At a children's choir workshop at Tabor College, Mable Boyter, a leading children's choir director, said that children should be exposed to music that they can "grow into and not out of."

One thought that continually haunts me is that a child's experience in music and attitude toward music should be limited by his own capacity, not that of his music teacher or choir director. We dare not lightly decide the musical or spiritual potential of any child. We must consistently teach music in such a way that each child becomes aware of music as an art, and that he be given every opportunity to discover the spiritual force of music to its fullest and develop his musical aptitudes as much as possible. To do otherwise is to be a church music leader without integrity.

One of the bright spots of the Christian education program in America has been the development of graded choirs. This program has given another opportunity to teach children Bible knowledge, doctrine, Christian living, and in some ways church history.

The children's choir program is one of the first places where Christian service is taught and experienced. Each time they perform they are engaged in Christian service. Unusual evangelistic opportunity is given as children recruit other children to the program. A specific outreach is extended to homes, as parents fellowship together through choir activities and are attracted to the services when their children sing.

During my first year as minister of music, I organized a junior high girls' choir and scheduled it to sing once a month in an evening service. As a part of their training they sang service music using various responses in addition to the anthem of the evening. At the end of the service when the altar call was given, I noticed a father and mother come forward to accept Christ. After the benediction, as I turned to direct the choir in the closing response, a girl with tears in her eyes excitedly whispered to me," "Those are my parents." In this case the parents came to hear their child sing, and ended up making a decision to commit their lives to Jesus Christ. Years later while visiting this church I was informed that the mother was teaching a Sunday school class. That experience was a great spiritual stimulus to me as well as to the girls in the choir.

The children's choir program is important to the individual child because singing in a group helps him develop a sense of poise and self-confidence. He becomes a part of a group and realizes that a choir requires team effort. He gains a sense of responsibility and cultivates dependability. Furthermore, he finds ways to contribute to the total cause of the choir, which in turn promotes loyalty, self-control, respect, and consideration for one another. Here, too, he acquires a sense of stewardship as he develops a respect for church property, robes, music, and instruments.

The graded choir program gives a child the unique opportunity to discover and present spiritual truths in an appealing and beautiful way. He learns to identify and have spiritual experiences with music. Throughout his whole life this will open new opportunities for him to communicate with God. From these choirs will come the future song leaders, pianists, choir members, directors, church music leaders, and parishioners who use, understand, and experience music to the glory of God.

The Minister of Music

The growth and success of a music program in a church lie basically in the effectiveness of the work of the minister of music. This person may devote his full time to the music program of the church. In most cases he is a part-time choir director, organist, song leader, or other music leader. No matter how extensive the responsibilities may be, how small or how large the church, the success of the work depends primarily upon its leadership.[7]

Those who predict the demise of the organized church feel that individual leadership will not be essential in the future because the strength of leadership will be invested in the group. It seems to me, however, that regardless of the cohesive status of a society, certain persons always take on greater responsibilities and emerge as leaders. It would be a misjudgment in strategy to neglect leadership training for

---

[7]Consult the following resources for additional reading. Austin C. Lovelace and William C. Rice, *Music and Worship in the Church* (Nashville, Tennessee: Abingdon Press, Revised and Enlarged Edition, 1976), pp. 51–69.

Ray Robinson and Allen Winold, *The Choral Experience* (New York: Harper's College Press, 1976), pp. 44–52.

Vic Delamont, *The Ministry of Music in the Church* (Chicago: Moody Press, 1980), pp. 27–33.

all phases of church work. I am particularly concerned with the problem of the minister of music because no other human factor is as important to the success of a church music program. Too many church music programs suffer from inadequate leadership.

What are the ingredients that enhance effective leadership in a church music program? Ordway Tead defines leadership as "the activity of influencing people to cooperate toward some goal which they come to find desirable."[8] The following qualities of leadership are delineated in his book. I'll try to adapt them to fit the setting of the minister of music.

A Sense of Purpose and Direction

It is said, "The world stands aside to let pass the man who knows whither he is going." A choir will rally quickly around a choir director if he shows with persistent clarity and definition the purpose and direction of the choir program. It is important that the choir members see the same purposes and goals as the choir director. Each member should realize that his part is important and that the choir as a whole benefits by learning, practicing, and struggling with the director.

Physical and Nervous Energy

To be a leader means to experience a tremendous nervous energy drain. Choir directing demands a conspicuous vitality, spark, and exuberance to inspire the choir to a high level of performance. A visibly charged and spirited director will generate similar feelings in his choir.

Enthusiasm

All good purpose and direction needs to be energized by enthusiasm. Directors who approach their work with intellectual detachment and a cold academic attitude will

[8]Ordway Tead, *The Art of Leadership* (New York: McGraw-Hill, 1935), p. 20.

alienate choir members instead of attracting them. Choir members must see that the choir director is excited with his work, his music, and his choir. There is no substitute for enthusiasm that can give spark and dynamic to a choir.

Friendliness and Affection

It is true that "out of the heart are the issues of life." Choir members will be open to being led if their director communicates love for them. Jesus had great success because He cared for people and because He felt deeply and with great affection for those who followed Him. Friendliness, appreciation, and respect are the wellsprings that bind a choir director to his choir.

Integrity

Mutual trust must be felt by the choir members for one another and toward their director. For the director this means living a consistent Christian life outside the choir loft so the choir will know that he truly believes in the principles he upholds. The choir members must feel confident that their director will not betray their purposes nor give up when the going gets difficult.

Technical Mastery

If his leadership role is to be long lasting and significant, the choir director must have acquired an adequate technical mastery of music. He must know how to communicate all necessary elements of music while conducting, understand how to analyze various music styles, have a reasonable understanding of the techniques of singing, and have a broad acquaintance with church music and literature. I have often observed people with attractive personalities and seemingly good qualities for music leadership who eventually fail because they are inadequately trained as musicians.

Decisiveness

All groups expect results. A feeling of accomplishment and activity must prevail. Decisive character is indispensable; to flounder in indecision is disastrous for a choir director. President Woodrow Wilson stated in a conversation with Lincoln Steffens:

> In an executive job we are dangerous, unless we are aware of our limitations and take measures to stop our everlasting disposition to think, to listen, to not act. I made up my mind long ago, when I got into my first executive job, to open my mind for a while, hear everybody who came to me with advice, information, then someday, the day when my mind felt like deciding, to shut it up and act. My decision might be right; it might be wrong. No matter, I would take a chance and do—something. [9]

Upon reaching a point of decision, the choir director must act with confidence and without hesitation. The fear of making mistakes is natural, but it must be overcome. A director, for instance, must decide on the tempos, dynamics, and spirit of a number and then aggressively project these concepts while conducting.

Intelligence

We can do little about our inherited intelligence. Most of us, however, do not use our maximum intelligence and capabilities. In planning the music for a worship service or a choir program, we must use our best knowledge, judgment, intelligence, and common sense.

One of the important aspects of intelligence is our capability to develop ways of solving problems. At the outset, a choir director must develop through study, work, and experience a philosophy about his own approach to church music. Next, the choir director needs to regularly assess his ability to detect problems. It is essential to be aware of

[9]Quoted by Tead, p. 121.

when and where a problem exists, then to work with the causes rather than the symptoms.

I once heard a story of a test given to determine if a mental patient was ready to be released. The drain in a sink was plugged and the faucet was turned on. If the patient would get a mop, start mopping the floor, and let the faucet continue running, he was retained. If, however, he analyzed the source of the problem and turned off the faucet, he was released. In many church music programs, choir directors are not able to detect problems at their sources. In a sense they are mopping floors instead of turning off faucets.

Identify the problem and do something about it. If your problems are many and time is short, priority demands that you select the biggest problem first. Next, ascertain the cause of the problem. Caution must be taken not to look for a single cause; often other causes are interrelated. Once the problem and its causes are determined, a course of action must be planned. It is important that alternate solutions be prepared. Since our minds are finite and our information is always incomplete, we must be ready to shift to another plan should the first plan fail. Do not depend on trickery or gimmicks to give permanent results.

All of the previous considerations will be totally ineffective unless we put the plan into action. There is a time and place when we must confront the problem and do something about it. Here we need to exercise our greatest sense of diplomacy, call on our best sense of judgment, and depend upon the leading of the Holy Spirit.

Teaching Skill

It is obvious that a large part of the choir director's work involves teaching. The starting point is to inspire choir members with the desire to learn, for real learning comes from within. For example, it is better to have choir members learn to appreciate all types of anthems rather than merely tolerate certain kinds, for "A man convinced against his will is of the same opinion still."

A communication gap between the choir and the choir

director can nullify many previous teaching efforts. Choir directors must understand, especially when they are new to a choir, that the starting point for the learner is at the point of his own understanding and skill. A choir director often moves too fast for his choir. He should be careful that he does not get too far ahead of the choir, lest he make the mistake of the proverbial general in the Army who got so far ahead of his troops that they began to shoot at him, mistaking him for their enemy.

Faith

Our congregations are looking for a faith that will give assurance, enthusiasm, direction, and meaning. They want to be released from the shackles of sin that bring monotony, mediocrity, dullness, and a self-centered life. At this point the choir and its director can render a genuine service. Initially, much of this will depend upon the faith of the director.

A choir director must possess four aspects of this all-encompassing faith: in Jesus Christ, in himself, in the people with whom he works, and in music. The role of the choir director often involves a sacrificial stance. There will be days when he must stand alone, when some choir members may be turning away, when choir loyalties will be focused in other directions. To have the resources to stand with courage and strength in such times is most essential for a director. To have serenity and confidence in these moments is the mark of a strong faith. We are not left to bear our burdens alone in a spirit of discouragement and disappointment, for the Lord said, "I will never leave thee, nor forsake thee" (Heb. 13:5).

Results ultimately depend upon our attitude. When we lay bare our souls in complete openness, we must face ourselves honestly and identify our true attitudes. Each of the qualities mentioned for leadership should be tied to the two words, *I will,* for in them we will surprise and amaze ourselves at what can happen. If we do not accept this challenge, who will? We cannot—nor do we want to—evade the responsibility of being custodians of the glorious art of church music.